ARCHITECTURE in the Real World

ARCHITECTURE
in the Real World

The Work of HOK

by Walter McQuade
designed by Paul Grotz

Harry N. Abrams, Inc., Publishers, New York

Library of Congress Cataloging in Publication Data
McQuade, Walter.
Architecture in the real world.
1. CCC/HOK (Corporation).   2. Architecture, Modern—
20th century—United States.   I. Grotz, Paul.
II. Title.
NA737.C33M36   1984   720′.92′2   84-2881
ISBN 0-8109-1822-6

Published in 1984 by Harry N. Abrams, Inc., Publishers,
New York. All rights reserved. Copyright 1984
under the International Union for the protection of
literary and artistic works (Berne). No part of this book
may be reproduced without the permission of the
publishers.

Production by Chanticleer Press, Inc., New York.
Composition by Dix Type Inc., Syracuse, New York.
Printed and bound by Dai Nippon Printing Co., Ltd.,
Tokyo, Japan.

Foreword

During my years as an architectural observer (for *Fortune, Architectural Forum, The Nation, Life, Connoisseur,* and others) I have increasingly wanted to get behind esthetics to describe how an architectural firm functions, what makes it succeed, beyond talent and taste. In other words, I've wanted to go past the facade into the business. To my knowledge, that has not been attempted before.

Three years ago I got the chance to try. One office, a large and able one, agreed to lay itself open to scrutiny, finances included, with no right to edit the results. It is an unusual office in some respects, not only larger than most, but ambitious esthetically and compulsively well run. Yet, in its problems and practice, it resembles the profession as a whole.

So, after several hundred interviews and a few thousand miles of travelling, I wrote this book. It may have some answers in it for smaller firms, or even bigger ones. At the least, it may pose them some interesting questions. Architecture is a strange profession, a precarious mixture of high art and canny business that is frequently lashed by economic suspense: when the national economy sags, building can go limp very fast, as all architects know, including those described in these pages.

Thanks are owed to many people. Chief among them are George F. Hellmuth, Gyo Obata, the late George Kassabaum, King Graf, and Jerome Sincoff—the latter two of whom, with Obata, are now the operating leaders of the firm HOK. I am grateful as well to many of their colleagues, who put down their drawing pencils or looked up from their computers to help: Robert Barr, Edward Bartz, C. Robert Belden, Donald Berry, Roslyn Brandt, Bernard Bortnick, Jerry Breakstone, Jamie Cannon, Frank Clements, Harry Culpen, Charles Danna, Jerry Davis, George Dickie, Robert E. Edmonds, Dorothy Forrest, Reagan George, James Gilman, Gerard Gilmore, George Hagee, Frank M. Hammerstrom, Velpeau Hawes, James Henrekin, George W. Hellmuth, Kathy Hoester, Charles B. Hook, Peter Hoyt, Scott Hueting, Lawrence Hultengren, Robert Hysell, Chih-Chen Jen, Herbert Koopmen, Kenneth Kosar, Dale Kostner, Marcia Lacy, Dennis Laflen, Richard Lapka, Donald Lee, Patrick MacLeamy, Charles McCameron, Robert Messmer, Catherine Moutoussis, James Moynihan, Virginia Miller, Rolf Muenter, Neil Porterfield, Charles Reay, Bill Remington, Terril Richert, Timothy Rickard, Terryl Rodrian, Chester Roemer, Susan Sanner, Larry Sauer, Larry Self, Gary Silver, Robert Stauder, David Suttle, Jody Taylor, Richard Tell, Nancy Toffant, Tad Tucker, Kathy Ulkus, Kiku Obata, William Valentine, Paul Watson, Graeme Whitelaw, Hugh Williamson, Henry Winkelman, Kathy Wolfe, Masao Yamada, Floyd Zimmerman. Lorrie Adair, of the HOK office, executed most of the drawings.

Assistance was given, as well, by a number of clients, Gerson Bakar, Roger Boas, Michael Collins, Raymond Nasher, and Rawleigh Warner among them. A thank you is due to the leave committee of Time Inc., who, with the generous concurrence of Bill Rukeyser, Managing Editor of *Fortune,* granted me leave of absence for the journey. Thanks, too, to the photographers whose work is acknowledged individually on page 230, particularly George Silk, who believes that pictures of buildings should contain people. Most of all a warm thank you to Paul Grotz, a colleague of many years' standing who designed the book, but —as always with Paul—did much more than that to carry it forward. What is wrong with it must be blamed on the author alone.

Baiting Hollow, Long Island
Summer 1983

Contents

CHAPTER ONE

Architecture in the Real World

At the top of an aluminum and glass office building in downtown St. Louis, the professionals who staff the home office of Hellmuth, Obata and Kassabaum, Inc., having arrived at the office at 8:30 a.m., are going calmly about their morning's work. Among them are 70 registered architects, 19 planners, and 23 mechanical and electrical engineers, as well as landscape architects, interior designers, model makers, specification writers, computer professionals, graphic designers, accountants—in all, 237 men and 101 women of HOK's nationwide staff totalling 711. Boatmen's Tower is the name of the building, and HOK not only works in it but in 1974 designed it, taking for itself the 21st through the 23rd stories as well as parts of three other floors.

On the 22nd story, in his office just west of the tall-ceilinged drafting room, Gyo Obata huddles round a table with a trio of HOK designers; pencils in their hands, rolls of tracing paper before them, they are threshing out the most effective floor plan for an Exxon research laboratory on the East Coast.

In an office across the drafting room from Obata's, a small loudspeaker for the moment dominates; a conference call is under way. Three ranking HOK staff members, Chester E. Roemer, Tad M. Tucker, and Chih-Chen Jen sit around the receiver listening intently as a voice from 7,000 miles away describes problems that the HOK construction office in Saudi Arabia is having with footings in the desert. The home office experts ask questions and argue some points briefly among themselves. Then Roemer puts their advice together into clear instructions.

On the floor below, King Graf, national market-ing director for HOK, is discussing the prospect of a large commission for an urban skyscraper with Jerry Sincoff, chief administrator of HOK, and senior vice president Gerry Gilmore. Graf and Sincoff are both vice chairmen; the designer, Obata, is chairman and president. The three make up the office of the chairman.

And still another floor lower in a quiet office sits George Hellmuth. Technically, Hellmuth resigned as Chairman of the Board in 1978 at age 71, turning in his stock and yielding control. But he now functions as Chairman of HOK International, a wholly owned subsidiary, and still drives his Chevrolet station wagon into the basement garage each morning, parks it beside Obata's BMW 530i, and rides the elevator upstairs to work. Just now he is mulling HOK's chances of getting an assignment to design a large national hospital in one of the new African countries.

From their windows, HOK employees look out at an interesting and varied neighborhood. Due east lies the Mississippi River, with its lofty and serenely soaring arch. Three blocks to the west is Louis Sullivan's great Wainwright Building of 1890, and directly across the street to the south crouches the old Federal Court House, where the Dred Scott decision was first delivered in 1850. But intermingled with such landmarks are recent structures, many of them the work of HOK. On Pine Street a brand new HOK office tower is rising, headquarters for Southwestern Bell; toward the river is the CBS Gateway Tower, while even closer at hand, just past the Court House, stands the Equitable Building, an HOK office slab that is completely mirror-walled,

*< King Saud University in Riyadh, Saudi Arabia
under construction*

and that reflects the far side of the Court House dome back toward HOK's windows. On its ground floor the Equitable Building also, as it happens, contains the restaurant Anthony's, with darkly glimmering interiors by HOK: Anthony's is illuminated solely by the suspended brass lamps that Alvar Aalto originally designed for the Savoy Restaurant in Finland, and is a very suave place to lunch a potential client.

HOK is almost as deep into the architectural grain of its home city as Aalto is in Helsinki, having produced not only office buildings but public and private schools, research plants, a planetarium, even a herbarium for the Botanical Garden. It has buildings in many other big U.S. cities as well. Two years ago in San Francisco alone, for example, it saw to completion the Levi Strauss office complex (750,000 square feet of space), a new five story Saks Fifth Avenue on Union Square, and Moscone Center, an enormous convention facility for the city. HOK has also been involved outside the U.S. in work valued in the billions.

HOK's rivals are the other big national firms that turn out quality architecture: Skidmore, Owings & Merrill, I.M. Pei, Kevin Roche, Edward Larrabee Barnes, Johnson & Burgee, Mitchell & Giurgola, Harry Weese, Murphy-Jahn among them. Year by year these and a few other professionals build what is best in the new American cityscape. Their structures and spaces interest and rouse us, standing out from the blur of merely commercial buildings, which offer little beyond air conditioning and profitable rentals; yet there are those who say the good buildings are often indistinguishable from the bad.

Like other vocations, the architectural profession contains a mixture of the nobly aspiring, the rapacious, the discount hacks, and the solid middle-of-the-road practitioners.

Counted in dollars, building is probably the second biggest business* in the country. Yet there are

* Next to food.

only about 65,000 architects as against 440,000 physicians and 500,000 lawyers. This is because architects are not responsible for buildings in the same way that doctors are responsible for medicine and lawyers for navigating the American legal maze. Architects bear somewhat the same relationship to building in general as clergymen now bear to the marriage ceremony; both have lost much of their influence over these specialties, officiating in perhaps half of all relevant situations.

As a result, not only are architects few in number, but the average architectural firm is small. The latest census of U.S. business, made in 1977, found that there were just 11,346 architectural firms in the country. The American Institute of Architects estimates that the average number of employees (including proprietors) is between seven and nine people—and is even smaller for those firms that are not affiliated with the AIA. Overall, 92% of AIA's member offices employ five or fewer professionals. The average annual gross income from fees in 1977 was in the neighborhood of $262,000 a year; with the inflation since 1977, however, the figure today is probably closer to $400,000.

HOK is not an average architectural company: in one recent year its total gross billings approximated a million dollars a week. In addition, it offers a wider spectrum of services than most architects, performed by the array of professional specialists mentioned earlier. Yet its basic product remains buildings. So, like all the other architectural companies, it has to deal with two major problems.

The first is the business problem. When the economy dips and corporations and institutions are forced to retrench, one of the first items to vanish from budgets is the building program. In such troubled periods as the early 1980s, hundreds of architectural offices simply disappear, many of them never to return. Compared with the average firm, HOK is well armed against recession; it is big, and it has a lot of momentum and a strong marketing department. But it is by no means immune, so it deliberately maintains a kind of permanent nervousness about booking business, in good times as well as bad.

The second problem is more recondite but in its way just as pressing. It is the design problem.

The profession today faces a real dilemma in dealing with the architecture of the recent past. The customary chronology in all the arts is a chronology of rebellion: the young rebel against the old, today rebels against yesterday, until in due course the present supplants the past. But this usual course of events becomes awkward following a period of such extraordinary creativity as occurred in architecture during the early and middle parts of this century. The 1920s through the 1960s saw the most complete revolution of the building art in all of history, even greater than the changes wrought during Romanesque and Renaissance times. This revolution was led by a group of remarkable designers: Frank Lloyd Wright, Le Corbusier, L. Mies van der Rohe, Alvar Aalto, Walter Gropius, the Saarinens, Louis Kahn, and a few others.

Architects today can be described as still bobbing in the wake of these tremendous ships. A generation of talent has had to take over from a generation of genius, and finds the going a little problematical.

One way out of the bind has been not to rebel at all, but simply to accept the style that overturned architecture 50 years ago and to carry it a few inches further. Thus, there are architects today whose work is almost more like the original Corbu than Corbu's was: surreal, spectral white houses and gleaming small institutional buildings that appear to be floating off their sites, in defiance of gravity or the rules of perspective. The effect is elegant but a touch lapidary; when the forms are honed down to such a sere, refined state, they can lose the lyrical edge of that very tense kind of architecture.

A second, briefer approach to the design dilemma has been by way of paradox, perhaps even parody; if this is not to be an era of breathtaking new buildings, perhaps it can be an era of witty ones. It was in this spirit that a group of architects about 15 years ago appropriated the lay public's own folksy vernacular, exactly as the Pop painters had done earlier on canvas. Favoring millwork from common lumberyard catalogues, neon signs from Main Street bars, welded chain address posts and the like, they learned to emulate the flavor of a roadside drive-in or a spec builder's bungalow, but in suavely proportioned structures. These designers are ironists, and they have been interesting in a literary way, but a little blank architecturally.

Then there are the new historians. Operating first under the general title of post modernism—a title they've since grown tired of—they have been rummaging among stylistic techniques of such earlier designers as Andreas Palladio for devices to incorporate into their otherwise rather conventional modern buildings: architecture for fun. When a prestigious architect such as Philip Johnson has played this old game the results have been sometimes astonishing: a gigantic glass skyscraper in Pittsburgh designed with a Gothic silhouette for Pittsburgh Plate Glass, or in Houston, a bulk with acknowledged Dutch massing for the Gerald Hines Interests, or in the Manhattan financial district, a blandly crenelated castle of speculative office space known as 33 Maiden Lane.

A recent variation of post modernism is called post modern classicism: so far most of its buildings look like bulky but frail papier-mâché stage sets, their bluntness broken up into surfaces with combinations of bright, childlike colors. Architect John W. Hartray has said about post modernism, "The movement looks as if it may pass into history without having made any."

Just peaking as this book goes to press is yet another movement that might be called neo-expressionism, although it too echoes the architectural past. The new expressionists include a number of talented designers who have made their way upward into positions of authority in firms that produce substantial buildings. They are impatient with most of what is—or is not—going on in architectural aesthetics, and are out to arouse some visual excitement with work that recalls the lyricism of the 1920s and early 1930s, when unique skyscrapers such as the Empire State and Chrysler buildings stabbed upward into the sky. And sometimes these designers succeed, with exuberant glitz.

They have chosen, however, a rather slippery style to reach back to. Art Deco, the name usually given to the dominant style of the 1920s, represented an attempt by jewelsmiths and architects schooled in the Beaux Arts tradition to come to terms with an emerging industrialism, and they designed some remarkably subtle, even poetic structures to bridge the gap between their own cluttered neoclassical youths and the spare modern style that lay just ahead. The result in architecture was romantic spires that continue to please the lay public, and that all but the most scornful modern architects have always really rather liked (if sometimes in secret). But today's designers are trained differently, and confront a different set of construction challenges.

There is the matter of craftsmanship too. I remember walking through the lobby of the Empire State Building one day in the 1950s with Frank Lloyd Wright. The master was wearing his cape and his pork pie hat, and carried his dapper walking stick. He paused several times to point the cane at some of the admirable details of the marble work. "We'll never see the like again," he remarked, and he was probably right. Though great architects are still being born, the world seems to produce fewer and fewer great craftsmen, and those that do appear generally become dentists. Construction tradesmen today can bolt buildings together quite efficiently, like cars—but no longer like carriages.

Most American architects currently in practice, however—and certainly most architectural firms—do not follow extreme or whimsical paths. True, they can still more or less feel Mies and Wright and Corbu looking over their shoulders, and they are also aware (if more faintly) of the great architects of the distant past. But their personal inclination, their training, and the preferences of their clients all conspire to propel them forward along the broad avenue known as functionalism*. These architects proceed from one commission to the next, influenced not so much by theoretical considerations as by what works well, in their own structures and those of their rivals. And through the scramble of their lives—the struggle to design good buildings and get them erected on time and within the budget —they gradually change and grow. One such firm is HOK.

* Louis Sullivan in 1918 defined functionalism in one of his "Kindergarten Chats": "Form ever follows function, a universal truth. The main function, so far as you will be concerned, will focus on the specific needs of those who wish to build, and such needs are quite apt to be emotional as well as what is generally called practical."

CHAPTER TWO

Beginnings

Many—probably most—architects enter their profession for reasons that go back to childhood.

As a schoolboy in San Francisco in the 1930s Gyo Obata, though both his parents were artists, was lured toward science, a subject he excelled in; but he recalls that as early as the sixth grade, when asked what he hoped to become, "For some reason I said I wanted to be an architect"—not the first gifted eleven-year-old to meld art and science and come up with that answer.

King Graf had a grandfather who was a famous planner, an uncle who was an architect and a graphic artist for a father: it seemed natural to him to choose the architecture school when he entered college. He did not really have to puzzle over it.

Jerry Sincoff's career began at the age of fourteen when his ninth grade project, the design for a house, won a prize at the St. Louis Science Fair. Then, four years later, the School of Architecture at Washington University awarded him a scholarship that took him through his first year. He worked his way through the rest, graduated, joined the rapidly expanding firm of HOK, and never looked back.

As for George Hellmuth, the man who started HOK, his original motive was something like Graf's; he early decided that the best thing he could do with his life would be to emulate his father, who was an architect. The senior Hellmuth had a comfortable practice in the city of St. Louis, specializing in business buildings, Catholic Church work, and the grand, old-fashioned mansions that in those days symbolized the good life for St. Louis's well-to-do burghers (and in recent years have begun to

do so again: many of the elder Hellmuth's fine old houses today stand refurbished and gleaming, gazing out from behind neoclassic white columns onto shady private streets).

All through the 1910s and 20s the Hellmuth family led a prototypical upper middle class life. In 1931, young George graduated from Washington University's school of architecture with a master's degree, the winner of a fellowship for academic excellence that paid for a steamship passage to France, a year's architectural touring, and matriculation at the École des Beaux Arts at Fountainbleau. But when the new *diplomate* returned to America in 1932, bringing with him his watercolors of European scenes, he found his chosen profession in a state of severe disarray. This was particularly true in St. Louis, a city already well past its prime by the time the great depression fell. St. Louis's golden years had been the half century following the Civil War, when it dominated trade along the Mississippi River, became one of the largest inland railroad centers in the country, and rose to fourth in population on the roster of U.S. urban centers. It coasted comfortably enough into the 1920s, but the 30s slugged St. Louis. Trade fell, industry languished, and building virtually came to a stop. In short, this was an appropriate time and place to learn about the vulnerability of small architectural offices.

In St. Louis in 1932, Hellmuth soon discovered, there were no positions to be had in private practice, even in his father's firm. He was luckier than some young architects, however: he wangled a job with the city as what was called a junior architect. He made working drawings for such buildings as police stations and bus shelters. Over a period of years, he also did a bunch of comfort stations—"about 25 of them," he remembers. "I'd do the whole job from beginning to end: design, working drawings, specifications, then I'd go out and supervise construction."

After seven years had passed in this fashion, Hellmuth, by now 32 years old, went to talk with his father again about the chances for private practice. But the answer was still discouraging. "No one in St. Louis knows how to practice architecture successfully," his father told him, "and that includes me. If you want to learn how, go to a big city, find a big office, and get them to take you on."

Detroit in 1939 was already stirring with the presentiment of the wartime boom to come; Hellmuth was hired as a draftsman there by Smith, Hinchman & Grylls, then as now a leading firm specializing in industrial buildings. Soon he found himself designing, virtually alone, a thousand-foot-long warehouse. But his engaging manner caught the attention of the head man, and it wasn't long before he was lifted out of the drafting room and given a desk in the "solicitations" department.

During the seven years Hellmuth worked for St. Louis he had formed lasting friendships with some of the young political hands around City Hall, and long after his move to Detroit and Smith, Hinchman & Grylls, he would take the train periodically to St. Louis and make the rounds of the municipal offices that had design work to farm out, hoping to win a commission from them. "How about giving some of those jobs to me to take back and do in Detroit?" he would ask winningly. His friends would have liked to comply, but had to turn him down as an out-of-towner. "St. Louis work stays in St. Louis, George," they told him.

Hellmuth remembered their words in 1949, when his first proprietorship came about. He, Minoru Yamasaki, and Joseph Leinweber left SH&G and set up a partnership with two offices: one in Detroit (called Leinweber, Yamasaki and Hellmuth) and the other in St. Louis (Hellmuth, Yamasaki and Leinweber). From the beginning the St. Louis office did land a lot of the local municipal work, including the design of Lambert Field, the city's airport terminal. And when the partnership split up in 1955, with Yamasaki and Leinweber staying on in Detroit, it came as no great surprise that Hellmuth chose to regroup in his home town, offering a 25 percent partnership in a brand new office to Gyo Obata, Yamasaki's deputy for design in St. Louis, and 25 percent to George Kassabaum, Leinweber's deputy there for production. For the time, he kept 50 percent of the partnership for himself.

To survive for long, a new architectural firm needs a strong sense of direction. From his postwar files at SH&G, Hellmuth saved a 23-page single spaced memorandum that he had written to the managers of that organization, telling them how he believed they could create a "depression-proof" office, and the fledgling HOK began life with that

George F. Hellmuth, left. Right, the leaders of HOK: King Graf, Gyo Obata, and Jerome Sincoff. Obata is Chairman and President, Graf and Sincoff are Vice Chairmen.

blueprint very much in mind. Its chief points can be summarized:

* Never depend on just one building type, but develop a battery of them—schools, shopping centers, libraries, hospitals, office buildings, prisons, etc.—to cushion a drop in demand for any one specialty.

* Diversify in location too: go where the work is, and set up branch offices. When the economy tilts down in any one part of the country, it may rise in another.

* Expand into architectural subspecialties, such as landscaping, city planning, interiors, industrial design, and graphics.

* Set up a thoroughly systematic marketing group to identify prospects, and contact them before they think of contacting you.

* Put effort and money into professional public relations.

* Organize the office for maximum efficiency by giving each of the three major partners a separate function: design, production or marketing.

HOK started with an office staff, not counting the partners, of 24 people and that first year took in gross fees, before salaries and other expenses, of $750,000. Its very first building was a handsome, carefully sited public school in a St. Louis suburb. Soon it won the commission for another school and after that a school and chapel on the outskirts of the city for a Benedictine Academy that Hellmuth's four sons attended. It was the chapel that brought HOK its first national notice, a structure with a thin, frail-looking concrete roof shaped, seashell-like, to

shelter the multi-altared layout—one altar for each Benedictine monk—that the order prefers.*

Hellmuth went after, and landed, enough other local work to keep the little office busy. In 1961 came the first really big commission, an entirely new campus for the University of Southern Illinois across the Mississippi in Edwardsville. In carrying out the campus, HOK established its very first branch office, just 15 miles from home. A year later Hellmuth sold enough of his stock to Obata and Kassabaum to make the three equal partners.

The partners attended to other items from Hellmuth's memo as well. To expand the firm's repertoire of building types, Hellmuth spent weeks in Washington, D.C. stalking the architectural commission to design a major federal prison in Marion, Illinois, and finally landed it. This was a job that was to lead to many more correctional institutions.

HOK's first corporate building of national scope was Obata's beautiful lab for IBM in Los Gatos; its first hospital was constructed in 1959, and in 1970 its first airport. Its planning, interiors, and graphics sections slowly took form and expanded.

The firm that started small in St. Louis 27 years before, by 1982 employed more than 800 people in nine offices, and was turning out more than a billion dollars of work a year.

Design is the end product of an architectural firm, yet not all architects work as designers. Part of the staff has to get out the drawings and specifications, and see to construction; another part must track down the commissions and the clients. Design, production, and marketing are the three basic tasks, which each architectural office apportion a little differently. At HOK the separation of powers has from the beginning been deliberately kept sharp and clear-cut. It has also been very much influenced by the personalities of the three original partners.

---

* Many thought the shell showed evidence of the departed Yamasaki's style, but Obata says that the late Pier Luigi Nervi, the Italian virtuoso of concrete, had more to do with it. The Benedictines brought Nervi in to criticize during the design stage on his first U.S. visit. Obata had planned a burlier, more angular concrete building. Nervi's influence resulted in the thin curved roof that enclosed the church. A similarly styled steeple admits rhapsodical daylight indoors.

CHAPTER THREE

Design

Gyo Obata walks rapidly into the remodeled warehouse office of HOK in San Francisco. Slightly slouched, slim at 60, with straight shoulders and a wide rib cage, he wears a pale Italian tweed jacket, unbuttoned, over a black knit polo shirt, tieless.

Passing the receptionist, he gives her a quick nod, and without breaking stride turns down a corridor, slipping off the jacket as he goes. At the doorway to his personal office—a spacious work room maintained for his use when visiting—he ducks in just long enough to toss the tweed quickly across the seat of a couch, then moves on to the office of Bill Valentine, his design deputy in San Francisco. It is ten o'clock on a Monday morning, and Gyo, with a three-hour plane flight from St. Louis behind him, is ready to work.

The job that draws him to San Francisco is a sizable one, a multistory speculative office building with 700,000 square feet of floor area on a prominent site in Oakland across the Bay, near the curved Kaiser Company headquarters. HOK San Francisco was chosen as architect because of its good track record, because it is handy, and because of Obata's name, yet Obata has never met the client, and certainly will not do so on this visit. There is too much other business to attend to during the day and a half he has allotted himself.

Accordingly on this first morning, Gyo visits the site in person, Valentine acting as his guide, then in the afternoon meets with his San Francisco architectural staff to discuss the office building. In preparation for his visit, these designers have put together models and drawings showing a variety of solutions to the disparate problems of local zoning, street traffic, interior circulation, and views, as well as alternative ways to pack in as much rental space as the situation will gracefully bear, making the building profitable for the owner without paining the neighborhood. Obata listens to what they have to say, ponders, pulls their schemes apart and puts them back together again in new combinations, all the time applying his greater experience with highrise structures to make the eventual building function optimally. Obata's working style is instinctive, decisive, and quick. Over the years he has learned to use all the HOK regional offices as if they were fingers on his spatulate hand, and his grasp is very strong.

Across the Bay in Piedmont, a house that Obata has designed for himself and his wife is under construction, and late in the afternoon he takes time off to drive over and inspect it. But the new office building is never far from his thoughts, and he soon discovers that the top floor deck of his future private home commands a fine view of the site in Oakland. He stands up there for some minutes, gazing toward the site, trying to decide what will work best —a symmetrical tower or a more complex combination of shapes, on the skyline now dominated by the Kaiser office.

Tuesday morning he rises at six o'clock, plays a hotly competitive game of tennis with a client, splitting sets, then presides over another design conference at the HOK office, and at three p.m. is off to the airport and St. Louis.

He is not home for long, however. Thursday of that week he spends in Dallas with prospective clients for a $120 million office and shopping com-

plex. Then the following Tuesday he flies to Nassau in the Bahamas to confer with a Middle-Eastern financier whose scheme is one of the bigger ones on HOK's drawing boards: a $300 million combination of hotel, offices, theater, and shopping for a U.S. city. The conference is in Nassau because it is held on the client's ocean-going yacht, and Obata and his assistants travel there by chartered Lear jet, bringing with them a big packing case full of scale models.

The weekend after that, Obata proceeds to London to meet with the same client again; then flies, via New York, to Cleveland to get final approval of his design for Sohio's $200 million home office skyscraper.

One of Obata's more interesting recent buildings is San Francisco's convention hall, an enormous space sunk into the ground south of Market Street, a single room without any supporting columns, 825 feet by 275 feet, large enough to contain five football fields. Roofed by immense concrete arches, the cavernous space does not become visible until you ride a long escalator down into it; then it is astonishing.

Obata is a little the same way, but without the convenient escalator. Although he talks cogently on many subjects, his conversation covers a large essential reserve. He is not at his best with words anyway, but with a pencil and drafting paper. Then his skills crackle. Give him a complicated problem of space and human traffic to solve and he will almost immediately sketch out an intuitive concept that takes care of every difficulty.

His speed still astonishes, sometimes dismays, his colleagues; he himself, however, takes it for granted. "When you've been in the business for 25 years, you learn to get down to the essence of a problem fairly quickly," he recently said. "Designing, after all, is only a matter of lining up a collection of variables, then simplifying them into a single concept. You look at them, and an answer just clicks in your mind." Some architects simmer their

solutions a long time, like slow soup. Some produce coolly and methodically, like computers, every step logical. Obata is instant, computerized soup.

Because of the sheer volume of HOK work, Obata has had ample opportunity to develop a single Obata style, yet to date he has not done so.

It is true, of course, that only a few architects working today are recognizable in their buildings in the way that Wright, Mies, Corbu, or Kahn were: I. M. Pei, when he designs in concrete, is one; another is Harry Weese ("I like Harry's work," says Gyo. "I think that he has a certain kind of humor in his buildings. He tries to impart more humanity"). And, of course, when a large expensive building features historical whimsy it can often be traced to Philip Johnson. But Obata's presence in his architecture is always discreet, and sometimes almost insidious. Some of his buildings are light and delicate, some are heavy and dramatic. Even the houses he has designed for his private use are reti-

The ranking designers of the regional offices come together periodically in meetings. Top left are Larry Self and Larry Sauer; next down, David Suttle, Chi Chen Jen, and George Hagee; then William Valentine, Harry Culpen, and Chip Reay; left, Peter Hoyt beside Gyo Obata. Below, Obata makes an image.

cent architecturally, faintly impersonal, not the *tours de force* most architects feel called upon to produce in such circumstances.

Obata has also used a wider variety of materials and effects than most of his colleagues. Back in 1961, when he produced his first corporate design outside the state of Missouri, the group of research buildings for IBM in California, he surprised the profession by specifying that they be built of redwood—most architects at that time would have chosen the more officious steel or concrete. During the same period he designed a residence for married students at the University of Michigan in the form, unusual then, of wooden frame town houses clustered round a little playground park (and had them constructed, for economy, by a house builder instead of a general contractor). From the beginning, however, he has used hard materials too. One of his first well known buildings was the chapel of thin concrete, its roof ruffled for strength, that he designed for the Benedictines in St. Louis.

About midway in his career Obata got very interested in handling the flow of a lot of people in large, crowded places—airports, shopping galleries—and he is recognized as being very good at it. Though most of his urban office buildings do not differ markedly in appearance from the gleaming, glazed towers and slabs of other designers, they generally perform better. Many of his suburban corporate groups achieve lyricism—Squibb in New Jersey, Mobil in Virginia, and his first job for IBM.

Obata is willing to do research and to take esthetic chances. Faced with designing a university for central Saudi Arabia, he was not content to conjure up cinematic settings appropriate to Gary Cooper and the French Foreign Legion, as some architects have done in reaching for an indigenous Middle East style. He sought out and found a valid local building idiom in that bleak, sun-scorched land, the Najd style, which features flat roofs with small windows, and—through the Ottoman influence—beautifully intricate fretwork balconies.

Obata is hanging his own version of them on vast prefab concrete facades.

One reason clients often cite for their hiring of HOK is the firm's reputation for holding to construction budgets—the result not only of pressure from the efficient HOK estimators, but of instincts inside Obata himself. Whether he is doing a large research center or a house for his own use, there is no reason, he believes, why he can't meet a reasonable budget if he has thought through the total design. In the case of a high rise office building, there are five major elements that he concentrates on: the structural system, the mechanical system, the elevatoring, the exterior wall, and "how you meet the ground." Get those five within budget, he says, and the cost of the building will be under control.

In dealing with the five, HOK's size gives Obata advantages. For example, when he needs curtain walls he talks the matter over with a curtain wall manufacturer, who he knows will be eager to help because of HOK's large number of current office buildings under design. " 'Okay,' I say, 'look, we've got 25 bucks per square foot budgeted for wall; what can I do to make it a different detail?' He shows me how I can put on a rounded, shiny, stainless steel trim that will create some reflectivity at the edge, and that won't cost much extra. He'll even make a full size mockup of our sketch, so we can judge it. Right now we're doing an office building in New Orleans, and we wanted a green granite wall. Well, we got together with a stone supplier, who located a green granite in India, had it shipped to Italy, where they cut it into one-inch-thick panels, highly polished, and we're getting that wall for $28 a square foot."

On Obata rests the load of an endless number of decisions governing a very wide range of work—probably a wider range in terms of different building types than is handled by any other single designer in the profession. Most of the other large offices employ a numerous flock of autonomous, coequal designers who, further, usually specialize: some in hospitals, others in office buildings, housing, or air terminals. But Obata, assisted by his trusty team of lieutenants, does them all.

The captain's relationship with those lieutenants reveals certain of his inner complexities. Inevitably an occasional designer will chafe at the Obata domination and leave, and Bill Valentine in San Francisco, who has been working under Obata ever since graduating from Harvard's design school in 1962, says he must always explain to anyone new coming to work that while Gyo is easy to get along with in most ways, "if Gyo wants to do something, we are *bound* to do it that way. We're bound morally, and we're bound in a business sense. And we *will* do it that way. We're not going to look for a way to go around it; we're going to do it, even if we happen not to agree with it."

Nor does Obata dispense much, if any, verbal praise to his subordinates; he seems unable to. Most of his design staff is used to this, but conversation aboard the happy ship becomes a little ironical at times. One designer who is familiar with the vigorous political infighting of other large architects' drafting rooms, where the young designers compete for advancement with knifelike ruthlessness, jokes about HOK. "It's not that way here," he says. "We're united. It's all of us against Gyo."

What HOK's rivals in the architectural profession at large question is the complete control that Obata exerts over so large a practice. He not only spreads himself too thin, they charge, he suffocates creativity in the staff.

Yet turnover among designers is lower at HOK than at most big offices. Obata dominates, often with great stubborness, but within that framework he can be surprisingly flexible. A designer who has been with him for the past seven years says, "Other big superstar architects I've worked for, if you show them their idea isn't going to perform well in a particular situation, they'll tell you, 'Do it anyway.' Not Gyo. He'll listen, and if you're sufficiently persuasive he'll change the design.''

Sometimes he rethinks a design for a client, too. Mobil Oil's chief executive, Rawleigh Warner, asked Obata to scrap a completed design for a headquarters office building in Northern Virginia after he had second thoughts about the elevator layout, even though the Mobil executives had already officially accepted it. Warner recalls, ''I said, 'You know, I really think we've got to start all over.' Gyo was absolutely marvellous. He said, 'All right, Rawleigh, that's perfectly all right, we *will* start over.' I thought that was extraordinary.'' The design was turned inside out.

One of Mies van der Rohe's most famous aphorisms was ''God is in the details.'' Frank Lloyd Wright's emphasis on ''organic'' architecture meant, among other things, that each small piece of a building, say the corner of a window, must match and share the character of the whole building. But the priesthood is a little different today, at least for most big time architects, of whom Obata is a conspicuous example. There are just so many hours in Gyo's days and nights; his concentration must be on the concept, with dependence on lieutenants to fulfill it in window trim and column facings.

Moreover the industrial efficiency of today's building product system, though helpful when it comes to shopping for granite curtain walls, also imposes certain limitations on architectural work. Wright's spirited structures retain his personal touch because they were virtually made by hand. Even the gem-like bronze curtain wall on Mies's Seagram Building in New York, though an epigram of industrialism, was custom crafted. (Seagram was also the first large U.S. office building with bronze-tinted glass windows; Mies had to coax the glass companies to try it.) But architects today must put their buildings together out of basically interchangeable parts—mass-produced costume jewelry. For these reasons, they are finding it harder and harder to control the tooth and texture of their work, a situation that pains them. Every architect wants to be a virtuoso, including realists like Obata.

Which may be why, at this stage in his career, Obata shows some small signs of restlessness. He talks about his recent travels in Europe, admiring the old architecture. ''The buildings have been touched by so many hands; there is so much activity in the finishes. We were brought up with a plain vanilla kind of detail. I think we are headed toward some of the other.''

Several of the buildings on HOK drafting boards, or standing around the various HOK offices in large model form, show a tendency toward the resonant lyricism of Alvar Aalto, a source seldom turned to by American architects. Aalto, off in his wintry Scandinavian lair, was a very functional designer, but even back in the 1920s he was using curves, rich natural materials, and shapes that evoke imagination, conveying a feel of the architect as individual craftsman and artist, not so tied to the real estate machine. One of Obata's Aalto-like models is an early study for the Sohio skyscraper in Cleveland, with a silhouette that steps back like a gigantic stairway in order to prevent its bulk from looming over the adjacent public square. In its final design the building still steps back from the square, but in a simpler and less interesting way, necessitated, Obata explains with a little shrug, by the demands of rental agents for large floors.

''Aalto was his own man, a very mature architect always, from the very beginning,'' says Obata. ''It may be partly a matter of schooling. Here in America it takes a certain number of years before you get away from the rectangular forms we grew up designing; we were trained to be very logical.

''Aalto broke that logic down and began to play with shape and space. The great poetry in architecture comes about in the breaking of logical rules. The question is, how to do that without jarring? It must be like Ella Fitzgerald singing—really smooth and supple.''

The Production End

HOK's ability to function as broadly as it does in its regional offices, yet still exert strong central control, rests on a different kind of design from that of architecture itself, and one of the men principally responsible for the pattern is no longer present. In the middle of an August night in 1982, George E. Kassabaum was awakened by a headache at his home in suburban St. Louis. He had suffered a massive cerebral hemorrhage, and three days later he died, at Barnes Hospital in St. Louis, age 61.

Kassabaum was a lean and limber man with many interests: he had served as a particularly forceful national president of the American Institute of Ar-

chitects; at the time of his death he was working in his off hours on a book about Marcus Aurelius. But his main preoccupation by far was HOK, and his steady hand is still visible in the firm's smooth operation.

Kassabaum was also close to the two members of the present executive trio who have succeeded original partners, King Graf in marketing and Jerome Sincoff in operations. George K.—as he was called in the office—first met Graf in the 1950s when Graf was a student and Kassabaum a teacher at the architectural school at Washington University. After graduation Graf went into service in the U.S. Navy, prowling the Pacific as an ensign on an amphibious landing craft. Landed in San Diego in 1956, ready to be demobilized, he was offered an enticing post as an admiral's aide in Europe if he would re-enlist. On impulse he telephoned his old design professor, now a partner in the new firm of HOK, for advice.

As Graf recalls with affection, George K.'s words were brief but effective. What he said was, "If you're going to be an architect, King, maybe you'd better begin." Six weeks later Graf was at a drafting table in the HOK office.

Kassabaum also selected and trained his own successor, Jerry Sincoff. Sincoff came aboard HOK in 1962 and for several years worked under Obata in design. But then he decided he would be both more useful and more fulfilled in the working drawing section, which was George K.'s domain. Kassabaum, impressed by him, soon made him a project manager on small jobs—"the impresario's job," says Sincoff—and Sincoff while still very young moved rapidly upward to become a top manager, heading the teams that have put up some of HOK's most successful buildings.

Along the way Kassabaum nurtured him, Sincoff says. "George K. gave people the chance to make decisions, which means the chance to grow," he says. "But when you had a problem, say with a consultant or client, you could always bring it to George to talk over. Usually you were the one who did most of the talking. He would listen, and listen, and then he'd pick out where the problem really lay."

Production is the specialized art of getting buildings built accurately, on time, and close to budget. This means processing the designer's art through the drafting room, making sure it passes zoning appeals, is safe, and will keep the weather out and the air conditioning in; providing accurate working drawings and specifications; and in general seeing to it that all minutiae are closely documented, with very little left to chance. These are the tasks that Jerry Sincoff has inherited as George K.'s designated successor.

But Kassabaum was more than a production man, he also served as his firm's chief administrative officer, and into this role Sincoff has moved more gradually. Should HOK go further into computerized drafting? How big should the bonus be this year? How does productivity per employee compare between HOK San Francisco and HOK New York? Which senior production man in St. Louis should be sent to head that department in a new out-of-town office? And on and on. These are intricate matters, and most of the decisions are really joint ones, arrived at after Sincoff confers with Obata, King Graf, and/or members of the management board.

With Kassabaum gone and Hellmuth relatively inactive, the structure of the firm has inevitably shifted in other ways as well. A group of proven younger architects has moved up to higher positions: Obata chose William E. Valentine to head all of HOK design under him, while Robert E. Stauder advanced in operations, under Sincoff, and Gerard G. Gilmore in marketing, under King Graf. Says Obata, "It is more of a team effort now." Besides Valentine, Gilmore and Stauder, the national specialty heads are Tad M. Tucker in production, Frank M. Hammerstrom in interiors and Neil H. Porterfield in planning.

Unlike some other big offices, Skidmore, Owings & Merrill for one, HOK does not operate on the "atelier" system, a term left over from the Beaux Arts past that means that separate design teams are set up within the office to take one building project at a time and carry it through from the very beginning to the dedication ceremony at the end. Instead, HOK has specialists in each stage of design and production who move in and out like offensive and defensive teams in professional football. Just one person stays with a job all the way, and that is the project manager, an executive architect who is responsible overall for everything, and who is the one HOK person, aside from the top partners, authorized to deal directly with the client. The project manager may have several buildings under his dominion at once.

When a job comes in to HOK, the chosen project manager is given a project designer and a project architect as lieutenants. The project designer, working under Obata, helps form the idea of the building, and once this has been approved by the client, evolves the detailed design, which also must be approved.

Now the project architect takes charge, seeing to it that others on the team bring the design along to the stage of final drawings, while the project manager oversees, answers questions, and after the contract documents are sent out for bid, arbitrates with the winning contractor. The project manager will also help evaluate subcontractors in some cases.

Then the contractors and subcontractors take away sets of the final design documents, and go to work making the shop drawings, which should show

how they plan to carry out the architect's design—what components they will purchase or fabricate and how they will put them together. At this point the project designer, one of Obata's deputies, reviews the shop drawings to make sure they comply with the original design intent. Then HOK's construction team moves in to observe the actual process of building, which, with a large job, can easily stretch over several years. Throughout the long process, HOK's computer center keeps each project manager up to date financially by means of a biweekly statistical analysis showing how his project is running in costs.

Among the time-saving production innovations at HOK over the years has been a streamlining of the drawing and specification process. This is important because an architect's profits usually depend on his or her efficiency in turning out working drawings. Compared with many firms, HOK relies less on formal, detailed drafting and more on performance descriptions—weathering and acoustical properties and the like. This saves time, thus money, and gets the job out faster for the always impatient client. "Show everything you have to on the working drawings, but not a line more," in the words of one HOK production chief.

Kassabaum once explained, "Contractors are always complaining that there are things on architect's documents that they never use, and that there usually *aren't* things on them that they wish were there. So, periodically it helps to get together with the construction people—not just the head of the contracting company or the estimator but with the guys out in the field trying to get the building up—and we review the whole situation with them.

"Take a window, for example. For an architect to sit down and detail each window on a window wall can be a terrible waste of time. The wall, of course, must fit the spacing and proportions and performance standards. But for a draftsman to have to draw in the clips for each glass section is unreal.

If he has to do that, what he does, naturally, is call a manufacturer, tell him the performance standard and ask, 'How many clips will we need?' And the manufacturer's answer will be accepted as gospel by everyone concerned. So why draw it?"

Another way in which HOK has quickened production tempo is by encouraging the use of analytical freehand sketches on drawings. In most architectural offices, these rapid, vivid explanatory diagrams are sketched routinely by experienced people, then given to juniors to draw up formally at the drafting boards. At HOK the freehands are often executed a little more completely by the seniors the first time around, with more dimensions indicated, and then simply printed on the construction documents.

The biggest advance in eliminating tedious drafting, however, has been accomplished through HOK's move into computer land. After experimenting with various electronic machines and techniques for about ten years, Jerry Sincoff in 1981 set up a computing center located in a newly rented suite of offices in Boatmen's Tower in St. Louis. Its staff of twelve, most of them trained architects as well as computer experts, operates a million dollars' worth of equipment and can produce some remarkable documents through their own copyrighted program, called HOK DRAW.

One example of adeptness is three-dimensional perspectives. In a matter of minutes HOK DRAW can print out perspectives of an office building indoors and out to predict what it will really be like when built; variations in the design can then be tried out quickly, and checked from many angles. Working drawings also can be routinely produced, compared rapidly, and edited, with the computer replacing a drafting table.

Another copyrighted program, HOK SPACE, is similarly invaluable in defining a client's spatial needs and processing raw information into efficient furniture layouts. Charts and graphs are apple pie for the clever electronic machines, and Sincoff uses

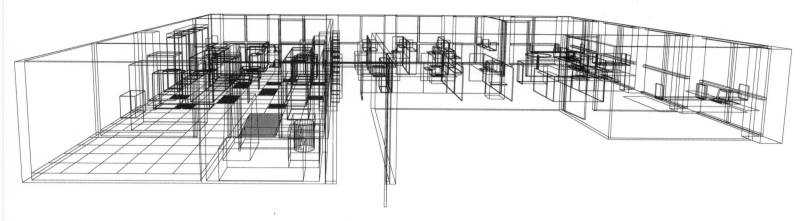

A cut-away perspective of the HOK computer offices in St. Louis. The drawing was made by one of the computers.

them to help handle administrative tasks as well.

Though all the outlying HOK offices are linked to the St. Louis computer center, the Dallas, San Francisco, and New York offices are also installing equipment of their own, each with a full time specialist to operate it.

Recently the regional offices have been granted a greater degree of autonomy in the matter of spec writing as well—which means the selection of materials and manufacturers for a given job, and which has long been the exclusive province of the central spec staff in St. Louis. Sincoff says, "An office with

90 employees, some of them young—and that describes most of our regional offices today—needs someone immediately at hand who is highly experienced in how building materials go together, how they move, whether they shrink or expand, and so forth. So last year we decided to add a specifications desk to each office, to work in constant contact with the specifications desk in St. Louis. They will be able to modify certain specs, for instance to compensate for regional climatic differences, provided they can make a good case to the central office." To quicken the interchange, a network of word processing machines connects all the regional spec desks with the central one in St. Louis.

At the end of his first year as chief of production and administration, Sincoff paused to take a breath and look about him.

It had been a busy twelve months. Moving into Kassabaum's shoes had been challenging enough. In addition, the timing of his ascension was difficult: that summer of 1982, the firm of Hellmuth, Obata and Kassabaum, which had grown steadily for 26 years, even during the economic recession of the early 1970s, suddenly faced the prospect of a straitened future.

Like other well run companies, HOK attempts to monitor its future by means of economic forecasting techniques. It closely follows the national predictors of business activity, such as F. W. Dodge reports, and each three months requires the heads of its various departments and regional offices to forecast their own profits or losses for the coming half year, based on current work load, plus new jobs that can be gauged with 90% certainty to be coming in.

By early fall of 1982, although there were a lot of large projects still being worked on, almost no new ones were in the offing. Sincoff, Graf, and Obata for the first time took action to shrink HOK. "We dealt with it the best we could," says Sincoff. "We had to trim our sails, which means cutting people and overhead; it was not a lot of fun." Within weeks, the total number of regular employees was reduced from about 800 to 700, while HOK's net fees dropped from $40 million in fiscal 1982 to a little more than $36 million in fiscal 1983.

Certain HOK offices suffered more than others. St. Louis, as part of the battered Midwest, home of the smokestack industries, was especially hard hit. HOK's San Francisco office, by contrast, did not have to lay off a single employee. On the east coast business dwindled in Washington, D.C. but actually picked up in New York. Houston faltered. Dallas stood firm.

Most American architectural offices, large and small, had even rougher going than HOK; some foundered in this worst of business weathers since the 1930s. Sincoff attributes his firm's relative success to two factors. "First," he says, "we have never been a swollen kind of firm. We've always been on the lean side more than the heavy." The second factor, he says, is more important: "We've made the conscious effort over the years to diversify our architectural services—architecture, interiors, planning, et cetera—and also building types: not just office buildings, but hospitals and correctional buildings and all the rest." This, of course, harks back to the long-ago memo that George Hellmuth wrote at Smith, Hinchman & Grylls in the 1940s.

"One reason San Francisco did so well," Sincoff adds, "is that it was not heavily into office buildings. So therefore, when some of the office buildings went on the shelf, there was a counterbalance to replace them, a corrections complex or other state job. Overall nationally, our interiors group had been doing about 12 to 14% of our work; during fiscal '83 it went up to 16 to 17%."

Sincoff summarizes, "I feel the firm pulled together very well. No large crevices opened up. There was no cracking or straining. There was a coalescing around what we are about." Even in the worst year, 1983, HOK showed a profit, though a very reduced one. And as of the fall of 1983, the forecast for fiscal 1984 was showing a rise in net to between $38 and $40 million.

CHAPTER FIVE

Marketing

Three hours' drive south of St. Louis, on a wooded ridge in the Ozark hill country, a burly man dressed in old hunting clothes stands tensely with shotgun at the alert, peering into the underbrush. He is all but motionless; only his lips move, as he cries out a strange gabble. Wild turkey is the quarry, and the only way to lure a male into range is to utter a convincing counterfeit of a hen turkey's converse.

All at once there is a faint stir in the underbrush. The hunter's eyes glint, and he feels a twinge of gout in one of his feet, but still he doesn't flick a muscle. Fifty yards away an ungainly fowl has begun pushing its bulk of feathers tentatively through the leaves.

As the moments pass, the turkey works its cautious way closer. At last it is just within range. Then the snap of a twig springs its wary instincts, and it is suddenly up and away. Once in the air it is as elusive as a quail, despite its mass. The hunter has his gun up and on it—BLAM!—and misses.

"Dammit," he growls.

George F. Hellmuth, Fellow of the American Institute of Architects, licensed to practice architecture in 15 states and the District of Columbia, may have missed one more wild turkey, but in the more than fifty years he has spent stalking business, remarkably few commissions have gotten away from him. Seventy-six years old now, he remains a legendary bagger of clients—"the granddaddy of architectural marketing," in the words of one of his young assistants.

It was Hellmuth, of course, who built up HOK's potent marketing department, in part by sheer force of personality. He is earthy, flamboyant and aggressive, traits useful to a salesman, as he himself began to realize back at Smith, Hinchman & Grylls in the 1940s, when he first left design behind him for the excitement of chasing commissions. "Sure I know a lot about design, I've won prizes in it," he said a few years later. "But I never really pleased myself with what I designed. I would rather use what I know to select a damned good designer, then go out and land the jobs for him."

The great salesmen of architecture have been diverse types and of no particular fame outside the profession: the greater public probably still thinks of architecture in terms of Stanford White and novelist Ayn Rand's Howard Roark, advocates and symbols rather than the flesh and blood professionals who get contracts signed. Only very occasionally does the almost religious aura of the superstar architect include the essentially calculating talents necessary in doing business. There have, however, been some well known teams of salesman and seer. In the late 19th century Daniel Burnham, of Burnham and Root, liked to say, "Make no little plans. They have no magic to stir men's blood," while pulling in one choice commission after another for his designer, John Root. And it was the steady, unflappable Dankmar Adler who found the clients for the protean exploits of his partner, Louis Sullivan.

Hellmuth's own aura is very down-home, and the older and more successful he has grown, the more he has come to resemble an Ozark possum in manner. After he nailed a mighty overseas commission several years ago, someone at a cocktail party asked him how he had done it. He responded with delight, "Why, I just put on my long-johns and waded in and picked up that pig and walked off with it!"

Beneath Hellmuth's joviality lies so much force that when he lets go he can be a little frightening. Within the firm he is famous for losing his temper and raging through the drafting room, and the late designer Charles Eames, who went to college with him, said he was a barbarian. With clients, however, a salesman of anything so expensive as architecture must be calm, pleasant and confident, and Hellmuth learned how to do that long ago. He amuses, he charms, on occasion he flatters outrageously. (When he was still a child a favorite aunt gave him a copy of Lord Chesterfield's letters to his son, from which young George learned the lesson, as he expresses it today, "Never underestimate the effect of flattery on even very important people.") And in the end, just enough of that inner force comes through to persuade clients that architecture is Hellmuth's obsession, and that perhaps it should become theirs as well.

Day by day there are two basic techniques for tracking down future architectural clients, and Hellmuth has always used a bit of each. The first consists of having assistants clip newspapers and following the commercial press to identify likely possibilities, then doggedly making contacts and keeping in touch. The other is more intuitive and proceeds by hunches, as when HOK back in the 1960s deliberately developed expertise in technical research centers, equipping itself to participate in the new wave of such corporate construction in the suburbs of industrial cities.

Because new clients can crop up almost anywhere, a master salesman has his eyes and ears constantly open. One time Hellmuth was invited by International Executive Service Corps to go to Egypt for a month to provide advice and guidance on the establishment of a design-construction company for high-rise steel buildings. Not long after his return, HOK received a commission to design a sizable office building in Cairo.

In devising strategy, Hellmuth takes pains to look at things from the point of view of the client, faced with the problem of choosing an architect. Especially when the client is a neophyte, third parties can be important; Hellmuth, therefore, has always gathered informal groups of lawyers, businessmen, bankers and the like around HOK, not only to advise the firm, but, by the way, to help nail down commissions. He also understands how difficult, and sometimes dangerous, it is for minor executives or government officials to pick an architect—so much money is at stake that if the building does not come out right, the pickers' careers may be seriously damaged. One way to reassure these clients is to avoid what architects call funky design: high style at the moment, but subject to rapid loss of charisma as the trends in architecture change. Anxious clients also feel better when their architect keeps in touch with them on a day-by-day basis, after the commission has been won and while the building is being designed. And, of course, what makes them feel best of all is to see their building get erected on time and on or near budget.

Architectural marketers, like other salesmen, gladly give up evenings and weekends for the chance to bag a major client; this is their sport, more exciting to them than turkey hunting.

Hellmuth takes an exultant joy in selling: "What I love," he says, "is making the kill, packing it in, and throwing it on the floor." He says that the greatest single selling opportunity of his life came along in 1974, toward the beginning of an economic recession that was to floor many U.S. architects. At that time HOK, in order to obtain a foothold in Manhattan, had recently merged with an old New York City architectural firm, Kahn & Jacobs. One September morning, a questionnaire from afar arrived on Robert Allan Jacobs' desk on lower Park Avenue addressed to Kahn & Jacobs/Hellmuth, Obata & Kassabaum, asking if the firm would be interested in designing a university in Saudi Arabia. Jacobs telephoned St. Louis.

Hellmuth swung into action immediately. First he caught a plane to Beirut, where he found a well-connected Lebanese lawyer willing to become HOK's advisor for a small percentage of the hoped-for fee. Then he flew on to Riyadh and began making friends. After 15 unsuccessful telephone calls, he arranged his way into the offices of both the Rector and Vice Rector of the existing old University of Riyad, and drank many cups of tea and cardamom coffee with them while discussing the problems and challenges of major university construction. His earnest advice: what they needed was an architectural firm with extensive experience designing big American campuses—such a firm as HOK.

When the university finally narrowed down its list of design candidates and issued formal invitations to submit credentials, HOK was among the 18 chosen.

In March 1975, the University asked just three of the architects to form teams consisting of themselves, one other architect, two engineering firms, and an architectural-engineering company from a prequalified list. Of the three architects invited to lead such consortiums, the only American was HOK. The second was from Austria and the third from Japan. It was becoming increasingly apparent that the commission would be huge: a university considerably larger than Harvard, to be built from scratch on a 2400 acre site on the northern outskirts of the Saudi capital.

Running his eye down the list of the prequalified, Hellmuth quickly picked four potential associates, all English-speaking, and invited them to form a federation to be called HOK + 4, and to be led by him.

The HOK proposal documents were delivered to the university May 1, 1975. At the suggestion of the graphics chief at HOK, Charles P. Reay, they were bound in magnificent folders made of Morocco leather dyed the royal green of the Saudi monarchy, packed in a suitcase of the same leather. The leather cost $4,000.

After nine months and a total of four trips by Hellmuth from St. Louis to Riyadh and back, HOK + 4 was pronounced winner of the $3.5 billion job under the longest contract—ten years—that the firm has ever entered. There was to be no recession for HOK (and no rest for Hellmuth's longtime assistant, Dorothy Forrest, a calm master of the process involved in obtaining passports and visas and all the other complex accommodations necessary to propel her boss and his troops around the world). Instead, over the next four years, HOK found itself hiring a lot of new people and moving into a lot more office space. It had to borrow $3 million to finance its expansion, but the Saudis pay their bills promptly, and the debt was soon cancelled. Today the university, named for the late King Saud, is rising on its crusty sand site on the northern outskirts of Riyadh. Meanwhile on the other side of town an immense HOK airport (Obata's masterpiece to date, in Hellmuth's opinion) is close to completion.

Among the many Arabs Hellmuth got to know during his trips to Riyadh is a prince of the royal blood named Abdullah, who happens to have received his education at St. Louis University in St. Louis. Hellmuth says, "I call him the St. Louis prince," and the two get along famously; the last time they met, Abdullah embraced him in a mighty bear hug.

The largest commission: above is the
presentation model for the $3.5 billion
campus of King Saud University in Saudi
Arabia. For the dedication the Saudi
rulers had a tent pitched, floored with
oriental rugs, on the 24,000 acre site
north of Riyadh. It held two leather
thrones for the late King Khaled and
Crown Prince Fahd, who succeeded
Khaled as King. Their retinue enters the
tent; Obata is shown behind the King
and Crown Prince; the King mixes
mortar to set the cornerstone.

CHAPTER SIX

The Regional Offices

HOK is not the only far flung American architectural company; a larger, older, and more famous one, now in its second fifty years and third generation, is Skidmore, Owings & Merrill. At its high point SOM had ten branches with a total of 2,159 partners and employees—including more people in its Chicago branch alone than the total count in all of HOK's offices combined.

HOK's system of regional offices, however, works very differently from SOM's. SOM might be likened to a fleet consisting of three gigantic aircraft carriers in Chicago, New York and San Francisco, plus a collection of cruisers working independently out of Denver, Houston, Los Angeles, Boston, Washington, D.C. and Portland, Oregon. HOK is a more unified organization, under stronger central control. It has cruisers too, in Washington, Dallas, San Francisco, Houston, Los Angeles, New York, Denver, Kansas City, and Tampa, Florida, but they all report to the command ship in St. Louis.

Abroad, both HOK and SOM maintain forces in Saudi Arabia, and HOK is active in Beirut, Lebanon, with a connection in Egypt as well. Compared with SOM most of the HOK regional offices are small (Gyo Obata feels a regional office becomes cumbersome if it grows past a staff of 150) and all are centrally supervised. SOM has no single design chief; HOK has, most emphatically. All HOK fees are forwarded to St. Louis for banking; all HOK paychecks originate in St. Louis. Specifications for materials in all the structures designed in regional offices come from St. Louis (although this practice, as previously described, is beginning to change under pressure from some of the regional offices).

Most of the special service departments in St. Louis have smaller duplicates in the other offices, but St. Louis still renders aid when needed—from Chip Reay with his two dozen graphics specialists, for example. Health facilities, criminal justice, and transportation all dock at St. Louis, although the larger outlying offices have their experts too in these intricate specialties. There is a lot of cross circulation of staff among all the offices.

One other significant difference organizationally between HOK and SOM is that at SOM there is active rivalry among the SOM branches. Those big SOM aircraft carriers have been known to launch strikes at one another; the SOM Chicago office recently completed an office building on the New York branch's home territory in Manhattan.

That kind of trespass is very unlikely to occur within HOK, where overall strategy separates the work geographically. Intramural competition is forbidden by the procedures manual, and King Graf keeps very good track of the marketing efforts in the various areas. Both HOK New York and HOK San Francisco are designing hotels in San Antonio, Texas, true, and the Dallas office is carrying out a large project in Middletown, Connecticut for Aetna Life & Casualty, but these jobs are the result of longstanding associations from the past.

HOK is just small enough for its leaders to control the outposts in a very personal way, and this easy intimacy is further abetted by the circumstance that so many HOK people attended the same college, though mostly at different times. Just 15 percent of HOK's registered architects are graduates of Washington University, but all the executive committee—Obata, Graf, and Sincoff—are. So are nine of the project managers, 13 members of the board of directors, and 52 of the 185 men and women with titles of associate or higher.

One Washington U. veteran in the St. Louis office is executive vice president Chester E. Roemer, who has been with the firm since its founding, and before that was with its predecessor, Hellmuth, Yamasaki, and Leinweber. Roemer's major role has been as project manager; he has a long list of buildings to his credit ranging from the first small schoolhouses put up by HOK in the St. Louis suburbs to the firm's biggest job to date, King Saud University now being completed in Riyadh, Saudi Arabia.

Chih-Chen Jen, who was born in China, graduated Washington U. in 1956 and began work with HOK the same year. He is a senior designer, and for several years he served as chief designer at HOK's New York office, before he was pulled back to St. Louis for a major role in the design of the vast Saudi project. He is also lead designer on a large international trade center HOK is building in Taiwan.

Two other veterans, both senior vice presidents, have rather different backgrounds, however. Tad M. Tucker got his bachelor's degree in architecture at the University of Nebraska in 1954, and operated his own architectural office for five years before joining HOK. Today Tucker is national director of production.

George B. Hagee's undergraduate and graduate degrees were both earned at Harvard. He joined HOK in 1956, and five years later became responsible for the programming and design of HOK's first really big job, the complete Southern Illinois University campus at Edwardsville across the Mississippi; and he has been heading big and small projects ever since, as a leader in design, master planning, and special architectural investigations.

Starting with St. Louis, all the carefully scattered HOK offices have something of the same look and feeling. Most of them occupy conventional office space, often in a building designed by HOK itself, and the light gray carpeted interiors are very much HOK in style. The desks are usually oak, with rounded edges and chrome legs. The files are wall-hung horizontals. Glass partitions admit daylight and afford views into the big central spaces, which are drafting rooms. In St. Louis the placement of the senior partners' offices emphasizes HOK's central preoccupation: design. Obata and Sincoff do not sit on the marketing floor, but upstairs right beside the drafting room.

Sincoff's office is neat, trim, efficient. Significantly he did not move into George Kassabaum's vacated quarters, which have been reserved for small staff conferences and still retain George K.'s orderly aura. Obata's office, by contrast, swarms with sketches, models, all the detritus of a designer in motion. The St. Louis *Post Dispatch* in a feature about the personal offices of important citizens once described Obata's lair as consisting of "a cluttered desk, walls, and tables overflowing with drawings of work in progress," and quoted its owner as saying, "I guess I really should do something about it." The reporter added, "Actually, he seems perfectly content with the way it is." Sitting in Obata's outer office, his secretary, Susan Sanner, makes everything work, down to ordering numerous lunches sent in for him and others. She has been known to set the phone down and sigh, "Sometimes I think we're running a restaurant here."

Of all the HOK offices, the most rapturous architecturally is HOK San Francisco. It occupies two vast top floors of a grandly burly old renovated warehouse that stands on the Bay waterfront below Telegraph Hill, just inland from Pier 27 of the Pacific and Oriental Terminal Company; occasionally the superstructure of a freighter rears up over the pier roof.

This is the kind of work space in which designers glory. Huge, arched plate-glass windows have been set into the bared brick walls, admitting so much light and view that an Easterner's eyes flinch. The two floors are connected by an unenclosed interior stairwell with a skylight above, so that daylight pours down into the lower floor as well. The framing is rugged timber, the wood-trussed ceilings soar.

Organizationally, the HOK San Francisco office has long been a mirror of the original in St. Louis in that it is managed by a troika of people with sharply defined specialties: Robert E. Stauder, the manager and head of operations; Patrick E. MacLeamy, who is in charge of marketing; and William E. Valentine, head of design. Terry Richert is head of production, Charles Whidden director of interiors and Floyd Zimmerman of planning.

The San Francisco office has always been allowed a good deal of autonomy because Valentine is probably Obata's most trusted designer. A native of North Carolina, Valentine went to the state university there, then to the Harvard Graduate School of Design, where King Graf in 1961 recruited him and two others from the ten-member master class. Says Valentine: "King looked at our work and didn't say much, but he had that deep, dark voice, and we just sort of followed him to St. Louis."

In sharp contrast to San Francisco, the Dallas office was first located in a 56 story Obata-designed building with mirror-glass walls, which, at the time it was built in 1974, was the tallest building in the city. It provided first class conventional office space, and the windbracing diagonals of the building's steel frame slanted across the window walls here and there with a Noguchi-like sculptural effect. Before long, however, the firm outgrew these quarters and had to lease the top floor of a nearby Holiday Inn for additional drafting space. Ultimately, the entire staff moved into larger offices in another new HOK-designed building.

King Graf is resident in the Dallas office, and the design head is Larry D. Self. Charles McCameron was also a designer, but recently asked if he could switch to project management and HOK agreed; it

The most important marketing people also have frequent conclaves, as do the planners, the production people, and the interiors specialists. Above, Gerry Gilmore and King Graf. Below, Jody Taylor, William Adams, and Robert Hysell. Bottom, Alan Shapiro, Robert Messmer, and, again, Jody Taylor.

is the firm's policy not to freeze people in one specialty if they want to try others.

There is a high proportion of Texans in the office including not only Larry Self, but also Velpeau Hawes, who is director of marketing. Hawes has served as president of the local chapter of the American Institute of Architects and is Graf's right hand man. A third Texan is Reagan W. George, a quiet-spoken graduate of Texas A&M who left a small local partnership of his own to join HOK two years ago. A number of HOK architects formerly had their own firms, successful enough but limited in the size of buildings they could handle. Within a week of arriving at HOK, George found himself project manager of a $230 million office building center in Houston, and now is head of production for the whole office. His presence on the staff, like that of the other Texans, has helped soften the feeling of the Dallas architectural community that HOK was a carpetbagger. HOK now has the second largest office in the city. Terryl Rodrian heads up interiors and Franklin Clements planning.

Graf himself may ultimately be called back to St. Louis, but right now he is happy in Dallas, and his presence is evident in many informal touches. HOK Dallas is less departmentalized than the other offices; for example, Graf decided it would be more stimulating to mix all the specialties together, with their drawing boards cheek by jowl. There have never been any corner offices at HOK Dallas, not even Graf's own; all the corners were made into conference rooms. The offices in the earlier skyscraper building contained two interior drafting rooms, one of which received plentiful daylight from the west, while the other depended on its fluorescent ceiling. The first was called the core by the staff; the second was known as the hard core.

The atmosphere in the Dallas office, as in all the HOK offices, is businesslike but informal, and once in a while facetious. Pinned to the tack board behind Graf's desk is an elaborately lettered scroll presented him at the 1979 office party: "Horace Kings-land Graf has been given this award for bureaucratic suavity. From your faithful staff."

HOK's system of regional offices was originally the idea of George Hellmuth, who sometimes had to overcome resistance from his partners, and who from the beginning cast his eye on two cities in particular. "You simply have to establish a real presence in New York and in Washington," he said. "Too much significant work is going on there to be among the missing."

But rather than start up cold, as was done with the other regional offices, HOK entered New York and Washington by affiliating with prominent local firms.

The reasons go back to early struggles in Dallas and San Francisco. At the beginning, the first big jobs in the HOK Dallas office were interiors, not buildings, while HOK San Francisco in its early days subsisted largely on work drawn from an alliance with an architect in Alaska: Crittenden, Cassetta, Cannon.

At that time in Alaska there were but few local architects, and the cost of building was roughly one and a half times what it was in San Francisco. As Bill Valentine explains, "If you could get an Alaskan fee for a $15 million building, and do the design drawings in San Francisco where the same job would have cost only $10 million to construct, there would be a reasonable profit in the work for everybody." So Valentine travelled north periodically and brought back suitcases full of assignments. HOK still is executing work in Alaska, though it no longer has an outpost there. Within the entire HOK network today, if one location is slack and another desperate with work, the transfer of some tasks can make for an economical balance.

Hellmuth entered New York City strongly, he thought, when he engineered a merger in 1972 with Robert Allan Jacobs of Kahn and Jacobs, one of the city's old established firms. At the time of the merger, however, the bottom had temporarily dropped out of the office building market, Kahn and Jacobs' specialty, and there was not much new work in the office. Worse than that, it soon became evident that this was not to be a placid marriage; Obata began having serious differences with K&J designers.

Obata doesn't like to argue. He resolved the difficulties by moving the office from its old digs at 2 Park Avenue to Rockefeller Center, which did clear the air, though at a cost of about a million dollars in rentals and remodelling. In the move the dissenting designers were designed out, and the Kahn and Jacobs name also disappeared from the logo. Bob Jacobs, an imposing customers' man, a big game hunter of note, and a fixture at the 21 Club, stayed on until early 1982, when he retired.

Dispatched from St. Louis to the New York office, meanwhile, were Gerry Gilmore, who took over management, and Chih-Chen Jen, who became lead designer. William B. Remington, HOK's national head of public relations, made the move east as well.

Manhattan Island to this day remains a slight dilemma for HOK. It is a notoriously inhospitable place for an outside architect to penetrate: the local professionals comprise the biggest and best organized segment of the entire AIA, and they play a very cagey game against invaders.

There is, for example, only one Frank Lloyd Wright building in the city. LeCorbusier has nothing but the exterior shape of the UN General Assembly; otherwise it was turned into a caricature of his original idea by local architects. Aalto is represented only by an interior. Mies van der Rohe's Seagram Building is probably the city's finest office structure, but a local man, Mies' junior collaborator, Philip Johnson, cleared the way for it.

HOK New York has scored very well in its work for clients beyond the city. In 1973 it designed for E. R. Squibb & Sons a world headquarters and research laboratory in Princeton, New Jersey. It is responsible for a large urban office complex in Pittsburgh, One Oxford Centre. There is work in Connecticut, and a recent commission is a headquarters for Grumman on Long Island. But in Manhattan itself, although HOK has been among the finalists on many major projects, its only completed building to date is a branch of the Greenwich Savings Bank on Lexington Avenue, a prize-winner but not a skyscraper.

George Kassabaum once leaned back in his chair, hands laced behind his head and speculated amiably: "We've been bridesmaids on three major New York projects, and we've been finalists, short-listed, on another ten, and all we've come up with is one local commission. Do you suppose there's no way a couple of country boys from St. Louis are going to invade that turf?"

Today the top designer in the HOK New York office is Harry Culpen, the production chief is Jerry A. Davis, and director of interiors is Roslyn Brandt and of planning Hugh Williamson, while the manager of the office is a native Australian named Graeme A. Whitelaw, who previously practiced architecture in his homeland, in London, in Saudi Arabia, and in such American offices as I. M. Pei and Philip Johnson in New York.

Under this leadership, and despite the city's recent lull in architectural commissions, the office is running strong, making money. Last year it won an enormous commission from AT&T, a group of buildings twice the size of the new AT&T headquarters by Philip Johnson being finished on Madison Avenue. The only drawback, for HOK's Manhattan ambitions, is the AT&T location—northern New Jersey. Nevertheless, as Harry Culpen says, with a smile, "It's kind of nice that the New York HOK office is helping along St. Louis." Significantly, Gyo Obata recently renewed the lease on his Manhattan apartment.

HOK established a marketing office in Washington, D.C. in 1968, then, in order to expand to a full service office, in 1975 merged with a leading local practitioner, Mills & Petticord. The National Air and Space Museum, designed in St. Louis, seemed a very strong entering wedge in the District as well, but business developed slowly. This regional office has run at a loss, and, unusual for an HOK operation, has also suffered several changes of direction. One head of design was offered a partnership in an out-of-town firm and departed. His successor in Washington showed too many traces of post-modernism to fit into the HOK functional tradition, and soon departed too. Larry Sauer is now design director in Washington and Marcia Lacy of interiors.

Despite its difficulties HOK Washington (Mills & Petticord has faded off the letterhead) has turned out some very deft jobs, including the alteration of Eero Saarinen's Dulles Airport terminal to accommodate the increased passenger and luggage loads of the wide-body jets. Obata's solution was a gracious one, done with deference to the fine Saarinen building. The office is currently at work on a commission coveted by many architects, a new headquarters for the World Bank.

Elsewhere the pattern of expansion continues. In Denver, where HOK has already completed one towering office block, Wesley Horner, a planner by specialty, is building up a regional office, with Jamie Cannon as director of marketing. The company's new Los Angeles regional office has enfolded an older HOK outpost in nearby San Diego. HOK now also has a Kansas City office, and a new one in Tampa, Florida, with the veteran Edward Bartz in charge.

Overseas an HOK+4 construction office in Saudi Arabia is currently involved in building the gigantic university outside Riyadh, and for several years there was an office in Beirut; the firm is now moving into the Far East. Graf says, "With our World Trade Center going up on Taiwan, a big one, we should be ready for some more projects in the Far East and Southeast Asia. You can't get business in Hong Kong if you locate in Singapore, but we think you can get business in Singapore if you locate in Hong Kong, so that's where we're going."

HOK has also been affiliated with an architect in Stuttgart, Germany, and has taken part in a developer group in Egypt that has produced a 20 story speculative office building in Cairo named—what else?—the Nile Tower.

Meanwhile, legends persist within the HOK staff concerning a future branch office in Zurich, with a woman as director and a Rolls Royce as office car. This possibility, including the lady but excluding the car, actually was contemplated in the late 1970s but nothing came of it. There was, however, a Rolls parked for several months in one of the HOK slots at the Boatmen's Tower garage in St. Louis. It was left there by a European-based consultant of HOK, and was finally shipped back to him in Paris, after the partners decided that a Rolls did not fit the firm's image.

CHAPTER SEVEN

Buildings Plus

Architecture nowadays is only the edge of the building axe; much of the heft derives from a combination of technical specialties—land planning, design of interiors, graphics, site analysis, and engineering of several kinds. Over the years HOK's St. Louis office has deliberately made itself competent across most of the board, and, on a smaller scale, so have some regional offices, particularly those in Dallas, San Francisco, and New York. The ambition of the company is to expand all other regional offices to the same level; meanwhile the skills can be sent out from St. Louis by team. In one recent year the company spent a million and a half dollars on air tickets.

Engineering has presented special problems. Because in certain projects the firm pays as much as 40 per cent of its fee to consulting engineers, some years ago it acquired a minority interest in a national structural engineering company, thus allowing a portion of these profits to return to the parent. Then in 1983 HOK decided to expand its own departments of mechanical and electrical engineering, specialties in which it had become particularly difficult to find outside consultants in some geographic areas, since many of the brightest young practitioners were focusing on high tech industries rather than buildings. Under the lead of vice president Larry E. Frank, the HOK engineering group is now large enough to function as a major component of the firm, taking on commissions from outside companies; its more basic purpose, however, is to pull back some of the usual consultants' fees—amounting in one recent year to $10 to $12 million—into HOK's own cash flow. Also the engineers can ex-

ploit the HOK computers, providing quality work, and fast.

A principal difference between HOK and some other large architectural offices is that not only are the major specialties in design, beyond basic architecture, available in-house, rather than contracted out, but the people who head the special departments sit on the HOK management committee and/or board of directors and thus can argue at a high level for attention.

This means a lot to all the specialists. George Dickie, whose department is land planning and landscape architecture, came over from the same kind of position with another large national architectural office, "not because I was acutely unhappy there: they used me well and treated me well. But my work was a secondary thing to them, whereas HOK is genuinely committed to the planning and landscape group. Neil Porterfield, national head of planning, is on the board and helps make policy."

Several of the HOK regional offices have survived sparse early years mainly through interiors work, an important and profitable part of design, and a very useful economic hedge during business recessions, when many clients decide not to put up that new building after all but to redesign the old one instead. Interiors jobs pay fast, too. They usually can be finished in a year, rather than the two or three years it takes to put up buildings. Fees, billed monthly, are arrived at by keeping close track of actual costs, then multiplying the resulting figure by a factor to allow for overhead and profit. Nationally, HOK's interiors group is headed by Frank

Hammerstrom, and in 1982 it was listed in *Interior Design Magazine* as the fourth largest designer of interiors in the country, with $132.2 million worth of work during the previous year.

Terryl Rodrian heads interiors in the Dallas office. A 1969 graduate of the University of Cincinnati, she came to Dallas in 1970, headed, she thought, for San Francisco, the preferred city for many designers, but on the way was offered a job with HOK Dallas. She accepted it, liked it, and stayed on.

Interior design completes architecture, Rodrian says: "It means taking the shell of a building and making it work, matching up the inside motifs with the outside.

"I was once present while a design jury deliberated in an interior design contest," she goes on, "and one of the jurors, an architect, complained, 'But how can I judge the interiors? I can't tell where the architecture leaves off and the interiors begin.'

"I was kind of shocked. That's how it should be. Interiors are at their best when you can't tell where the architecture leaves off and the interiors begin."

She will probably not move on to San Francisco. She has risen to become a senior vice president in the firm, has taken over responsibility for interiors work in Houston, too, and has married a local stockbroker.

Both the interiors department and the planning and landscape department execute numerous commissions that have no connection with HOK building projects; 40 percent of the people in planning, according to Neil Porterfield, are occupied with such outside jobs as devising a master plan for the city of Doha in Qatar, planning a private developer's 3,000-acre residential community near Salt Lake City, doing a study for an entire new town of 2,000 acres in Kuala Lumpur, Malaysia, or laying out a 2,300-acre mixed-use—retail, office, and residential—area near Kansas City. The HOK planning division, 50 strong, is larger than most independent planning offices across the country.

When HOK planners turn in a good job it often follows that the client seeks out the same firm to execute architectural commissions as well, a profitable dividend. For example, HOK planners and landscape architects were engaged in 1976 to make a comprehensive development plan for Lake Placid, N.Y.; out of it came the commission, two years later, to design the Olympic Arena there. Currently planner George Dickie is working on rural office parks near Washington, D.C. for two separate developers who each intend to put up about two million square feet of office space on large acreages just outside the district—quite a marketing prospect for future HOK architectural services.

Neil Porterfield has been with the firm for 19 years, and in the earlier ones used to upset George Hellmuth by his willingness as a private citizen to testify at public hearings against the development of such areas as wetlands, sometimes by potential HOK clients. Porterfield recalls with a smile that after he had spoken out against one U.S. Army Corps of Engineers project, "George told me I was a snotty-nosed kid. But I said that I knew I was right, and the truth would come out in the end."

In the Dallas office a typical planning job was recently carried out by planner and landscape architect Frank Clements, just down the hall from Terryl Rodrian. Clements' assignment was to advise Aetna Life & Casualty on the exact siting for its new offices, to be constructed in the Connecticut countryside 15 miles south of Hartford.

Aetna had purchased 287 acres, and Clements and his group produced a 40-page diagnostic breakdown showing different possible uses for each part of the parcel. First the total acreage was analyzed in terms of road access from existing and planned highways in that part of Connecticut. Then the parcel was separated into six potential building sites and a detailed study was done of each, based on landscape forms, vegetation, slopes, soil borings, utility easements, climatic variations within the micro-climate, and not least, the possibilities for long views across the landscape. With all the facts and figures in, the best site both esthetically and economically became obvious: on high land overlooking the countryside, with ample flat areas nearby for parking, away from drainage problems, in a location allowing development of the rest of the site into a rural park.

To give them further latitude to seek out their own clients, both the planners and the interiors division at HOK were established as independent subsidiaries in 1972. Three years later, however, they were reorganized back into the corporate fold. "The separate companies never quite found their own destiny," Porterfield puts it. Besides, he prefers being part of the corporation because then he sits on the central management committee, where he can function as an ecological conscience of sorts for the entire HOK product.

Another HOK design specialty cuts across the grain of the whole organization and characterizes it in important ways, not only to the clients but to the staff itself. This is graphics, a department headed in the St. Louis office by Chip Reay. One day last July Reay's staff of twenty was working on a typically mixed bag of assignments: designing signage for the Sohio Building in Cleveland, programming a historical exhibition for Washington University Medical Center in St. Louis, turning out a poster for a local Japanese kite festival, and picking colors for HOK's renovation of the old St. Louis Union Station, which the firm is transforming into a shopping-hotel-office complex. Last year it was Reay's team that selected and assembled photographs for an exhibit of HOK works that the firm was invited to hang in the Royal Institute of British Architects gallery in London. The first such invited display of an American architect's work at RIBA, it afterward traveled on to Rome. Graphics is not a playpen of design but a necessary adjunct for a large architectural organization, in effect the firm's signature.

Two newer architectural specialties were developed at HOK in the decade past, both of them providing services to U.S. corporations. One has since folded, at least temporarily; the other is flourishing as an HOK subsidiary.

The first, called Corporate and Industrial Services, set itself the task of helping an industrial company to upgrade its image and reputation in the community. It sprang out of an HOK planning project ten years ago, when the tide of environmental concern was running high throughout the land. The Dow Chemical Company of Midland, Michigan asked HOK's planners, for a fee, to take a searching look at its factories and other facilities in Midland and suggest ways of improving its industrial appearance both to its workers and to the rest of the city.

The assignment went to an HOK architect-planner named Jamie Cannon, who travelled to Midland, found the usual set of factories that had grown like grim Topsies to meet market demand, and brought some organization after the fact to them. He recommended that some unsightly functions simply be disguised by various devices, starting with landscaping. Berms of earth were built up to hide incurably messy operations, and certain passageways were rerouted to remove them from public view. Cannon also redesigned signs and fencing, and he cleaned up the existing architecture to a degree, too.

It was no small job, and before it was finished a dozen HOK people were working in Cannon's office in Midland. More commissions began coming in from other corporations who had heard about the program, and from several public agencies in Midland. At last in 1977 Cannon and his crew were called back to St. Louis and HOK began offering their expertise to all comers.

Cannon is now a senior vice president and member of the HOK management board, but he has moved to the Denver office, and the Corporate Services group has disbanded, a casualty of corporate budget-cutting of the 1980s. When prosperous times return, however, it is expected that Corporate Services will be reborn, and may ultimately offer HOK a major new growth opportunity, the chance to enter the lucrative business of factory building. The group had already undertaken projects for 28 of the Fortune 500 largest industrial companies in this country, including the design of service buildings—distribution centers, gate houses, fire stations, and the like—before the economy waned.

Program Management, HOK's latest new special service for corporations, grew out of one of those frustrating client episodes that sooner or later happen to all architects.

Several years ago a Midwestern food products company in Minneapolis wanted to expand its research operation, and hired a scientist-administrator to look into the matter. He and his engineering services department decided to build a new laboratory and decided also that HOK should design it. Jerry Sincoff became HOK's project manager, and everything moved along efficiently for several months. Working with the research vice president, Sincoff and the HOK team helped select a site, which was then optioned by the manufacturer's lawyers, and worked up schematic designs; finally they were invited to make what they anticipated would be a *pro forma* presentation to the chief executive of the corporation, who they assumed had been kept in touch with what was going on.

But he had not been kept in touch. At the end of the presentation this man, famous in the business world for his bluntness, turned to his research vice president and abruptly asked him if he had thoroughly investigated the possibility of expanding the company's existing research center downtown. Just as abruptly he called the presentation to a close, then hired a management consultant to make a study, the usual corporate band-aid procedure when blood has been splashed on the boardroom table. The V.P. soon afterward left the company.

"We didn't take it personally," the surprised Sincoff said afterwards, "although we were embarrassed for the V.P. But it was discouraging. We had used our energy, and theirs, and their money, and we were nowhere." He knocked the episode around in his head for several months, he says, and one day told himself, "We know about buildings, we ought to be able to help companies to avoid situations like this."

The result of these thoughts has been the development of a specialized advisory service called Program Management, now offered by HOK with great success to a few corporate clients.

Most large companies, thinking ahead into the future, make five or ten year contingency plans; these plans take into account changes that the corporation's top executives feel are headed their way—market opportunities to rise to, challenges to defend against. Sometimes the executives foresee that their product lines will be shifting. Or they may feel the need to further centralize their administration—or in some cases to decentralize it.

Most of these decisions are made on the basis of manufacturing, sales, distribution, or finance, and corporate managers today are, or should be, experts in all four of these areas. Few, however, know much about building. Moreover their building and real estate departments are usually quite far down the line in the corporate structure, and thus exert little influence.

HOK, through its Program Management section, charts the financial-architectural implications of the various choices faced by its corporate clients: if you make decision X, what kind of buildings will you need, and when? Most of HOK's program managers have degrees in business administration as well as in architecture, enabling them to relate more easily to executives from such companies as Motorola and Exxon.

Program management is a far cry from designing buildings, of course: were it to become simply a sales blitz for architectural services, it would lose its usefulness, and the client would be promptly put on his guard. Instead it might be called an exercise in architectural logistics, with the focus on very long term possibilities. Ten years hence the client may or may not be building new facilities, and may or may not want HOK as its architect.

A real estate inventory of the client's existing buildings and facilities—owned, leased, sometimes shared—is usually the first step. After that the game becomes more intricate, taking into account depreciation, federal tax policies, zoning, travel time between branch factories, the possibility of local real estate tax abatements, and the relative economy of revamping versus demolition and rebuilding, as well as many other considerations that ordinary architects rarely get involved in. The question, for example, of whether leased space is more economical than owned space certainly will depend more on interest rates for corporate loans than on any esthetic judgment. For that matter, the client in some cases may be best off vacating its leased space and subletting it, at a tidy profit, to another organization. HOK's program managers help corporations to make their minds up on many such business questions. An effective program manager proposes alternatives rather than unequivocal answers.

The firm's first client in the new specialty was the Ashland Oil Company. Scattered over various owned and leased quarters in and around Ashland, Kentucky, and getting cramped for space as it expanded into the coal business, the company engaged HOK to design it a new building, and Sincoff took the opportunity, with permission from the other HOK senior partners, to offer the new service, while also seeing to it that the commissioned building was delivered on schedule. He was accepted, and went to work on a major analytical report covering all Ashland's building options, as affected by both financial and operational considerations. Six months later he and his staff came up with six alternative scenarios for Ashland's physical consolidation, to take place not at once but in orderly fashion over a period of years. These were

pondered by the Ashland executives and their board, who then inquired about two other possible schemes; these too were programmed and run through the HOK computer.

Program management does not produce fast action, nor is it expected to, because of its long range anticipatory nature; it was a year and a half later when Sincoff's telephone rang in St. Louis with an Ashland executive on the line. "All right," he said, "we're ready to implement. We're moving out of downtown Ashland. We want your firm to help us decide on a site, remote but not too remote, where we can start assembling a new headquarters."

The site selected was in Lexington, Kentucky. HOK's planners analyzed it and developed a master plan, and so far HOK's designers and production people have completed the first two buildings. Already, says Sincoff, the client has moved out of almost all its leased buildings in downtown Ashland, subleasing the long term space on good terms. No time, money or effort has been wasted, he says; it has all been very orderly.

Program management, HOK is finding, can diverge still further from basic building, particularly when clients decide that HOK's staff is competent in a business way. One corporation, for example, wanted a new building to house its computers and wanted HOK to design it, but at the same time it asked the firm's program managers to help investigate the economic merits of purchasing computers, as compared with leasing them, as the company had always done in the past. Sincoff was soon at work in collaboration with the client's own computer department, which helped him devise a plan for purchasing add-on computers; instead of becoming obsolete after a few years, these can be kept up to date. The decision did not affect the design of the computer center architecturally, but it did constitute a major operational and financial shift for the client, which is really what program management is about.

In 1983 HOK decided to spin off the program

management department into a separate company, Corporate Facilities Planning, in order to demonstrate its detachment and place it on a par with other management consultants; the parent firm, however, retains ownership.

Most American architects today are giving a lot of thought to expanding their line of services. This is a subject much discussed in publications of the AIA, and HOK is currently mulling over several new possibilities.

An obvious one is the marketing of its copyrighted computer services HOK DRAW and HOK SPACE, a move that will probably be carried out by going into partnership with a computer software company that already has a staff of salesmen in the field. The customers would be smaller architectural and engineering firms that lack the capital to set up their own computer operations, but will probably soon need computerization of some sort to survive; there are so many of these firms that the program could be very remunerative.

Another interesting prospect at HOK is the possibility of putting together design-construction-finance teams to provide buildings—particularly hospitals and correctional facilities, in whose design HOK is expert—for municipalities whose tax revenues for capital expenditures are squeezed. "We could associate," says King Graf "with an investment banking company, and with a builder we know well; together we could finance the hospital or jail, design it, build it, and rent it to the municipality or state long term. The same process could work in the financing of corporate headquarters and research facilities for companies that don't want the buildings on their balance sheets."

Graf has also been pondering the architectural potentialities of the electronic manufacturing business. With all HOK's highly technical experience in building medical facilities and research and development buildings, he believes the firm can do well with the exotic and expensive structures necessary to semi-conductor manufacturing and the like.

Other paths taken by architects today arouse little interest at HOK, however. One is the possibility that the firm go public, selling stock in the financial markets. No one at HOK thinks this is going to happen. Obata, Sincoff and Graf all feel strongly that an architectural firm has to be owned by people who are architects first and managers second.

Another considerable lure is construction management. This is a post-World War II specialty that has sprung up to fill some of the gaps opening in the old client-architect-contractor relationship. Construction managers are expeditors and efficiency experts; they take charge of a job for the client and act as chief of staff by coordinating the diverse efforts of contractors, suppliers, architects, engineers, etc. Frequently CM companies are engaged even before architects are, which is one reason a good many architects are moving over to get into the business.

HOK's present instinct is to stay out of this specialty of managing other architects. The head of one of the regional offices offers a practical reason: "An architectural firm usually expands into this area at the peril of blurring what it really should be about. My feeling is that if you really have a good track record with some of the best CMs in the business, like we have had with Gilbane on the Air and Space Museum and the Lake Placid Olympic Center, why suddenly go into competition with them? Let's do our thing and let them do theirs, and have them look on us as a friend, and help us get design jobs when they are the CMs."

CHAPTER EIGHT

The New Marketing

It was Gyo Obata who steered King Graf into marketing. One day in 1959, when George Hellmuth by mistake had accepted two invitations to appear before building committees on the same night, Obata suggested Graf for the second appointment, took him away from his drafting table, packed him into a car with some sample drawings and photographs and sent him off to Paducah, Kentucky. Graf did not get that first job, but soon became Hellmuth's right hand. Today Graf leads HOK's highly organized marketing effort.

Sometimes he looks back to the 1950s and 60s, when successive building booms were reverberating through the national economy, and shakes his head reflectively at the ease with which Hellmuth, and he himself, used to go out and lasso commissions. In particular, he remembers the two of them in 1961 going up before a committee of business leaders in Winston-Salem, N.C., in the burnished board room of a bank—rich, clean, serious men attired in dark suits, white shirts, and somber ties, who had been charged to pick the architect for a new municipal convention center. Graf was also conservatively dressed, but Hellmuth had chosen to wear to the appointment what Graf recalls as "one of those God-awful neckties" framed by a bright red sports blazer, which had become rather rumpled during the plane trip from St. Louis. In the board room Hellmuth unbuttoned the jacket, leaned forward in his chair, and was soon making his pitch. He never has much liked showing slides. He thinks they are soporific. He prefers to sell by using magazine tearsheets of published jobs, which he spreads out on the table top, and lots of eye contact. He was fifteen minutes into his sales pitch when the chairman interrupted with a question.

"Hellmuth," he said, "where the hell did you get that red jacket?" Hellmuth murmured that his wife had given it to him.

"Well, I've got one just like it in my closet at home," said the chairman. "And tell you what: Now I'm going to *wear* it." A week later, HOK got the job.

Architectural marketing was simpler then. Today Graf heads a department that includes 17 representatives who spend the majority of their time in marketing and/or managing, though all are qualified architects or planners. Seven of the 17 work out of St. Louis (including four whose territories are nationwide), two work out of Washington, one out of Denver, three out of New York, two out of San Francisco, and two out of Dallas. The latter two are in addition to Graf himself, although he regularly ranges the world from Beirut to Hong Kong.

Graf says that today's clients, when shopping for an architect, are no longer satisfied to deal with just salesmen, they want to talk with the designers and the project managers as well, the people who will actually have their hands on the building. This means that Gyo Obata in recent years has become perhaps the single most important person in HOK's marketing efforts—paradoxically, for he is probably the least salesmanlike member of the firm. Obata's manner—quiet and unpretentious, lighthearted yet reserved—is not the stuff that makes for major architectural deals, at least not in the usual setting: a boardroom meeting held by the full executive committee of a large corporation. In the words of Gerson Bakar, the entrepreneur of the new HOK-designed Levi Strauss headquarters building in San Francisco, "He puts on the dark suit and the white shirt and stands up there with his slides, sure, but I would never pick Gyo to be my salesman in such a situation. However," Bakar adds, "get Gyo with the chief executive of that company, one on one, with a pencil in his hand, and it's a different story altogether."

Under the latter conditions "he's fabulous," says another San Francisco client, the city's chief administrative officer, Roger Boas, who picked Obata to design the huge municipal convention center. "I've watched him here in San Francisco, dealing with those who were opposing us on the convention center. He makes it appear effortless. He comes across as a fellow who doesn't have much responsibility, is a kind of simple, easy-going type, with little position in the world, a sort of fellow who's just shooting off the cuff on what he feels deeply about. Yet all the time he's got his facts so well organized that he's thinking many steps ahead of the client. His mind moves like mercury, and it's always exactly on the problem."

By far the most potent weapon in any architectural marketing effort, with or without skillful salesmen, is an endorsement by a former client, or by an independent specialist in building or in the real estate management business. One example of how the mere mention of a name can count is the way in which HOK was assigned the commission to design the Dallas/Fort Worth Airport complex in 1968.

This job had been virtually promised to a well known architect-engineer who already had the terminal pretty well designed* when the airport's sponsors decided to hire a new director: an assertive executive named Thomas M. Sullivan, who had participated in the building of JFK airport in New York, and who now insisted, as a condition for tak-

* and was later to be engaged to build it, or a near facsimile, in Tehran, a project that was aborted when the late Shah departed.

ing the Dallas job, that he be allowed to nominate the architect. Accordingly he asked his old friend, the late Wallace K. Harrison, who had masterplanned JFK, what architect would be best qualified. Harrison answered Kenzo Tange, the Japanese master, then added the name of Gyo Obata. Deciding that a St. Louis-based architect would be preferable to one working out of Tokyo, Sullivan called Obata, who flew down to Dallas, absorbed Sullivan's ideas intently, and impressed him.

Still, Sullivan had to convince his board of directors. He asked HOK for samples of its work, and Gerry Gilmore, the firm's senior vice president for marketing in St. Louis, flew down with an assorted parcel, arriving at Sullivan's office late on the evening before the board was to meet. When Sullivan unwrapped the material he was not satisfied with it. So at one a.m. Gilmore telephoned Graf in St. Louis, rousing him from bed; Graf put on his clothes, drove downtown to the office, assembled more material, and arranged for a chartered plane to deliver it to the waiting Gilmore. Gilmore recalled: "Just before seven a.m. I got it all over to the Republic National Bank Building in Dallas, where the board meeting was to be held. Sullivan was waiting for it. Then he went into the meeting.

"That was the longest 45 minutes I ever spent. Sullivan finally came out, looking very grim, and drove me back to his office, and told his secretary to get Obata on the phone.

"When he got him he said, 'Gyo, I just finished the presentation to the airport board. I'm sitting here with your guy Gilmore, and I'm afraid I've got some bad news for you.' A big grin spread over his face. 'The bad news is that I sold you to the board this morning, and now you're going to have to design this damned thing.'"

Satisfying a client does not always end with the construction of the building. It can go on, sometimes for months or even years after the dedication ceremony. Nine years ago HOK brought in an experienced construction administrator, Lawrence G. Hultengren, who had spent his previous career with the Army Corps of Engineers and the St. Louis County Department of Public Works. Hultengren spends most of his time roaming the HOK jobs under construction, but on days when there is a lull he goes out calling. He has a list of previous HOK clients, and he wants to learn from them how their buildings are working out. Just as contractors sometimes maim buildings in the act of putting them up, architects make mistakes too, and some are not apparent until the building has been in use a year or two. When this happens in an HOK building, Hultengren finds out about it on his tours, and if necessary will call back the contractor, as well as the HOK staff, to get the building fixed.

The firm is also very careful to rectify problems that crop up during the design or construction stage of a building, even if this means foregoing expected profits. "If you've committed a mistake, or if the design isn't satisfactory, you just have to be willing to lose money once in a while," Graf says. "We've had jobs where we've told our project manager outright, 'Look, we're going to do what we have to to produce the right results, and we won't hold you, Mr. Project Manager, responsible. It's not going to hurt your income, or your yearly bonus. This is a corporate decision, so let's get on with it.' "

These policies have cost the firm a few hundred thousand dollars over the years, but have resulted in an invaluable set of references to pass on to other clients.

A substantial portion of HOK's total architectural work load comes from three specialties: health care, mainly hospitals and medical schools; corrections, including very large prisons and other penal institutions; and transportation, which currently is a growing source of commissions—airports, subway stations, etc.

All the widespread HOK marketing people keep their ears open for leads in these building types, but in the home office in St. Louis are three men, administrators but heavyweight marketing people as well, each with a single full-time specialty.

In charge of health care is Jody L. Taylor, a trained architect who has been with the firm only since 1979, but who has nearly 20 years of previous experience with health facilities all over the country. Taylor explains some of the strategies involved in selling all three architectural specialties.

First, he says, hospitals and prisons and transportation centers—airports particularly—arouse a lot of civic passion from the moment they are announced: "You have to demonstrate to the client that you possess the political smarts necessary when dealing with communities, and also with administrative hierarchies."

Then, says Taylor, in order to seed referrals for other jobs in the future, the architect must keep in contact, and provide help if it is needed after the building is up, particularly if it is a health care center: "You don't abandon a hospital client."

In recent years HOK has been doing about $200 million worth of health facilities annually, for such clients as Duke University and the Veterans' Administration. About 70 percent of HOK hospital work is done in association with small architects who have the local connections that win them the job, but lack the staff (including experienced hospital designers) to carry it out alone.

HOK's first corrections job came in 1958: a maximum security prison in Marion, Illinois, which replaced Alcatraz. Since then the firm has designed many other penal buildings and is presently turning out about $150 million worth of corrections facilities annually, under the direction of architect Robert F. Messmer, who joined the firm four years ago after serving as chief of the Federal Bureau of Prisons' Office of Facilities Development.

Messmer holds that prisons and jails may comprise the most socially significant building type in which the firm is expert, because, he says, "They deal with failed people, and have to solve many,

many functional problems." This makes the building type one of the most expensive, often just as costly per bed as are hospitals. Currently correctional facilities, even tightly budgeted, as most of them are, cost between $90 and $130 per square foot, depending upon size. They have to be designed meticulously not only for security but for round-the-clock operation and that accounts partially for their costliness. (Including the expense of staffing, of course, prisons and jails are even more expensive to the taxpayers.) "They never close down," says Messmer, "or have slow periods."

There are persistent environmental difficulties in their design, too, particularly the noisiness inherent in such steely construction. The clanging of barred doors to cells can sometimes be muted somewhat by using very sturdy wooden doors. The walls—but not the floors—of general rooms such as dining halls are sometimes carpeted to diminish reverberation.

Most of HOK's correctional work is done in association with local architects, as in hospital work. "It is a depression-proof industry," Messmer points out.

The most recent of HOK's marketing specialists is its head of transportation facilities, Alan M. Shapiro. Transportation buildings are nothing new to the HOK repertoire, however. The firm has designed and built several notable airports—St. Louis's Lambert Field with Yamasaki, then, following that, the gigantic Dallas/Fort Worth facility, a regional airport in Lubbock, Texas, and the Dulles addition. The spectacular King Khaled International Airport in Saudi Arabia opened in the fall of 1983. They have also designed service buildings and airline interiors, and have planned airports that still await construction in Singapore and in Ecuador. HOK has done subway stations and rail service buildings on both coasts, too, and is remodeling St. Louis's old Union Station from a railroad facility into a shopping and hotel center. It is its ability to provide many different services, from regional planning right down to replacement of ashtrays, that makes HOK see for itself an important and continuing involvement in this expensive, difficult, logistical field.

Since the late 19th century in Chicago, skyscrapers have been regarded as America's outstanding contribution to architectural history, and architects compete intensely with one another to design them. These tall stacks of office space provide an architect everything he wants: challenge, fame, profit, a chance to be judged against other designers in the urban silhouette, even a kind of immortality. Skyscrapers generally outlive their creators; moreover, enormous numbers of people see and notice them, from the street, from other office buildings, even from airplanes.

Skyscrapers fall into two distinct classes. Most common are those put up by real estate developers, for whom profits generally come first and pride second. The order is reversed, however, when sponsorship comes from a large corporation that plans to establish its national headquarters in the building. This is the kind of job architects vie for hardest of all, as was recently illustrated by the dignified but hard-driving scramble for a commission in the city of Cleveland, Ohio.

The building in question was to contain 1½ million square feet of space, and would be the new home office for Sohio, one of the nation's largest oil corporations. Sohio (formerly Standard Oil of Ohio) is a venturesome but very systematic company. Its first step, once it decided to build, and even before considering architects, was to seek counsel from a number of real estate investment organizations. One of these was the Urban Investment and Development Company, Inc. Another was the Cushman Management Corporation, which in due course was asked to assemble a list of possible architects to design the building. After researching forty different firms, Cushman proposed eighteen as best qualified, all of whom were then sent a questionnaire.

HOK received its copy of the questionnaire on a Wednesday, and Gerry Gilmore glanced through it. Forty-six queries, covering everything from business references to the proposed fee, from statistics on employee turnover to esthetic issues such as what percentage of which designers' time would be devoted to the building. Gilmore knew at once that his department would be working through the weekend. Even so, it wasn't until the following Tuesday that he finally got the answers—150 typed pages of them—back to the Cushman office.

The questionnaire was used to weed out twelve of the architectural firms. Now just six remained for further consideration: The Skidmore, Owings & Merrill office in Chicago, Welton Becket in Los Angeles, Vincent Kling in Philadelphia, The Architects' Collaborative in Cambridge, Massachusetts, Cesar Pelli in New Haven, and HOK in St. Louis.

Sohio and Cushman's next move was to send a team out to visit the six firms in their home offices —a common practice today among big clients, who want to find out more about an architect than can be learned in a conventional boardroom presentation. When Sohio's team reached St. Louis they seemed impressed by the calmly busy HOK office, and they may have been additionally struck by the views out the window: like Cleveland, St. Louis is a waterfront city whose downtown, after suffering serious reverses for many years, is now making a strong comeback. In any case the visitors spent the entire day with HOK, further discussing some points on the questionnaire and getting to know Obata and Jerry Sincoff, who had been chosen as the managing principal if HOK were to win.

Not long afterwards Sohio announced it had narrowed its list of architects down to three—SOM Chicago, Welton Becket of Los Angeles, and HOK. Final selection would take place in Cleveland two weeks later, and each firm was to send no more than three representatives to meet the top Sohio executives. "It was made clear that this was entirely a chemistry session; we don't want your dog and pony show again," recalls Gilmore. Jerry Sincoff adds, "They knew we were all qualified. Now the top Sohio people wanted to see us and touch us, to find out which firm they could work best with over the three years that it takes to design and build."

All the meetings were scheduled for a single morning. The competing architects had encountered one another in outer offices in cordial rivalry on many other occasions. On hand were SOM Chicago's manager, William Hartmann and its ranking designer, Bruce Graham; MacDonald Becket, C.E.O. of Welton Becket, a persuader famous within his profession, accompanied by a pair of assistants; and for HOK, Obata, Sincoff and Gilmore. There had been a hint during the HOK office visit that Sohio was interested in combining store space with its office high-rise, so Obata brought along slides of the Galleria he designed for Gerald Hines in Houston.

Inside, waiting to meet the architects, were Alton Whitehouse, the chairman of Sohio, John Miller, the president, and vice president Webb Alspaugh; also Stephen Rigo, the Sohio executive chosen to ride herd on the project day by day, plus two executives from Urban Investment and Development and a man from Cushman Management.

Don Becket was first into the den.

Next came HOK's turn, and the interview began auspiciously. The exact site of the prospective building had not been revealed, but Obata, Sincoff and Gilmore had arrived in Cleveland the afternoon before, a chilly one, to walk around and absorb the flavor of the center city. Sincoff mentioned this, was asked what he and his companions had thought, and expressed the three's admiration for the old Arcade Building. The Sohio site, it turned out, was immediately adjacent.

Obata was asked if he thought a sixty story building would fit the site comfortably; he answered perhaps, but that HOK would want to consider alternative heights as well.

Slides were then shown of previous HOK work,

and the architects spoke of similarities between Cleveland and St. Louis, both of them old industrial cities with problems. They pointed out that Sohio's new building provided an opportunity to give a real lift to Cleveland, particularly if it was designed to weave its way into the city's street pattern and silhouette, not stand arrogantly aloof.

Throughout the meeting Obata did a lot of intent listening, as he always does, to the client's precise physical and budgetary requirements. Before it ended, however, he made a point of stressing that while HOK was eager to work on the building, it was important for Sohio to recognize that picking an architect was only the beginning; the corporation's own people would have to work hard too, if the project was to come out well.

Two weeks later Sohio asked to see slides of more work by HOK, which Gilmore hand-delivered to Cleveland. Then two days after that came the phone call: HOK had won.

There was one hitch, however: would Obata and Sincoff fly to Chicago to confer with Urban Investment and Development? It turned out that the firm's fee had been the highest proposed, so it was now shaded slightly to make it competitive. This is a fairly common procedure today: fees on major jobs are not taken as final until, as Sincoff puts it, "you get right down to the edge. Then they say, 'We want you, now let's discuss your fee.'"

The next time Obata went to Cleveland, it was to walk the site with Sohio's Chairman Whitehouse, and shortly afterwards HOK's planners and traffic consultants went to work on several siting alternatives. Their final proposal, accepted with enthusiasm less than a month later by the officers of Sohio, will not be 60 stories high but 44, deliberately leaving the old Terminal Tower dominant over Cleveland. The new building will also line up with an adjacent shopping street, and will step courteously back from Public Square as it rises.

A large table in King Graf's Dallas office is covered, day in and day out, with 40 or 50 piles of neatly stacked papers, each pile representing a prospective design commission. Usually about three out of four of the commissions are for buildings, perhaps one out of six involves interiors work, and one out of twenty has to do with planning. Many are the result of inquiries that come in to HOK unsolicited. The rest are split between new clients turned up by the marketing staff, and previous clients who are satisfied with HOK's past work and have come back for more. With over 25 years of momentum behind the firm—what Graf calls a track record—it doesn't get harder, says Graf, in some ways it gets easier. "But you can never relax," he says, "you have to keep going out there. The time to make friends is before you need them."

CHAPTER NINE

Architects and Money

"To an architect's clients, promises mean nothing," George Kassabaum once said. "To convince these men and women of action, architects have to conduct their own operation in a way that demands respect, justifies confidence, and maybe even rouses admiration. If you are running your office like a neighborhood shoe store, why should business leaders turn to you when huge sums of money are involved?" The HOK partners do not consider profit their first objective—almost no architect does —but they know they must operate an efficient and successful business enterprise. One reason is to reassure clients; another is to build up financial reserves and a good credit rating so the firm can keep going when times are bad.

Some kinds of architectural work pay better than others. Traditionally, the most profitable of all is a high-rise office building or a hotel; once the lobby and other public spaces have been taken care of, all that remains to be designed is a single story, which can then be stacked in layers to the sky, with only slight variations in the detailing. Office building clients are aware of this, however, and have recently begun narrowing the architect's profit on such projects. By contrast, a hospital, even a multistory one, is more complicated because it must house mechanical services that vary from one section to another. Hospitals require more technical study and more drawings than office buildings, thus earn a larger percentage fee—but not enough larger to make up the total difference in design time.

The only building type on which HOK has difficulty in making a profit is shopping centers. "We are sometimes approached by someone who has made a lot of money building strip shopping and now he wants to improve his image, to become a Jim Rouse," Graf puts it. "But when the time comes to set up a budget he frequently wants to cut corners to meet the competition. If he can save a nickel a square foot by putting in an ugly ceiling, well, who the hell looks at a ceiling? You're supposed to look at the merchandise! At HOK we're not very well attuned to this approach."

The kind of shopping center favored by the firm is the large complex that includes hotels and office buildings along with the stores, on the model of the Galleria in Houston, designed by HOK in 1965 for the Gerald Hines Interests. Says Obata, "If all developers were like Gerry Hines, we'd have better cities. He works with the architect: he wants to do quality buildings, and he'll pay a good fee for them. He is also a shrewd buyer. When he goes out to order a window wall, the supplier knows he's going to be buying five other major window walls in the coming year, and gives him a good price. Gerry saves money by exerting this kind of purchasing power, not by squeezing every penny out of a project, or screwing the architect into the ground." HOK designed Hines an even grander Galleria in Dallas, which opened in 1982.

By tradition, fee arrangements at an architectural firm are much the same as at an advertising agency: each of these organizations expends the client's money to produce something—a building or an advertising campaign, as the case may be—and each is paid a commission in the form of a percentage of the client's expenditure. An ad agency's fee is traditionally 15%, while an architect's is perhaps half that, depending on how big and expensive the building is. A house might earn a 20% commission, an office building 6% or less. The percentage tradition is fading in both advertising agencies and architectural offices, however. The ad men prefer to charge for services rendered, and so do the architects. This involves, usually, billing a multiple of payroll cost, or billing lump sum fees. A not uncommon way for an architect to present his fee to a prospective client today is by design cost per square foot of a building.

Overall, HOK aspires to a 15 percent before-tax profit on its net fees, but only rarely achieves quite that, and most years is quite content with 12 percent. When an architect's total office gross is $57.5 million yearly, as HOK's has been, a 12 percent before-tax profit is not small.

Big architects do make big grosses. When the magazine *Progressive Architecture* ran a feature on Skidmore, Owings & Merrill titled "SOM at Mid-life," it cited estimates that the company had billed between $35 and $50 million in fees during the previous year. SOM does not divulge financial details, but in the same article Gordon Wildermuth, managing partner of the SOM New York office, acknowledged that estimate as "a little low."

More likely it was quite low. A large architectural office should be able to count on about $50,000 per employee in billings, and SOM then had a staff of more than 2,000 people, including 34 partners, 93 associate partners, and 212 associates. Its gross for the year in question, in other words, was probably closer to $100 million.

When architects get into financial trouble, it is usually because of the way payments are timed rather than the overall size of the fee. Under the standard contract, a firm receives its first 15% on completion of the sketch plan, 20% more following finalization of the design, 40% when the drawings, specifications, and other contract documents have been completed, and 5% after consultation during the bidding process. The remaining 20% doesn't come until the building is finished, a process that can take several years.

The biggest part of the architect's profit, when there is one, comes with the 40% payment for contract documents; the financial trap is the final 20% for construction services. "Anything can happen during construction," says Sincoff, "bad weather, strikes, delays in delivery of essential materials, a collapsing contractor, you name it. But no matter what, the architect still has to pay his people, even though no further money will be coming in until construction is complete." He says that HOK is regularly approached by other architectural firms wanting to merge: "Usually they have several projects still under construction, with a lot of fee yet to be earned, and they aren't making their payroll. Things can get pretty grim."

Sometimes unexpected disasters raise the cost of the building itself, leading to argument and recrimination between client and architect. This is why in taking a job HOK is careful not to make too many promises. King Graf says, "We tell a potential client that we can minimize the financial risks inherent in producing a building, but we can't eliminate them altogether; the only thing we guarantee is a high quality building."

For architects themselves, the most feared disaster, short of a major malpractice suit, is a serious slowdown in the economy; among all the professions, they are the first to feel the pain.

Timothy Rickard started as an office boy at HOK in 1961, then went into accounting, becoming the company's first employee to take advantage of its education benefits program; eventually he rose to the position of director of finance. Rickard recalls that the first quarter of 1982 looked strong in predictions, but soon the firm's forecasters began to expect a major downturn, and as the season wore on, "Forecasts got bleaker and bleaker."

At HOK about 40 percent of total fees received goes to direct contract costs: labor, travel, and the like; another 30 percent goes to office overhead and

18 percent to corporate costs, leaving 12 percent for profit. That ratio of profit plummeted toward the end of 1982. It never disappeared completely, however, and by July of 1983 Rickard was able to announce that the forecasts for the new fiscal year begun that month were looking pretty good again.

Architects, individually, usually earn less than orthopedic surgeons or negligence lawyers; there are exceptions, however.

The writer remembers a dozen years ago having lunch at the Brussels Restaurant in Manhattan with a top-ranking partner from one of the leading New York offices and discussing income opportunities in the profession.

The architect volunteered that he and his equals in the firm would probably each draw about $200,000 that year. "But for God's sake don't let it get around," he added hurriedly, "I don't want any of my big-business clients to find out I'm making more than they are. They've got enough resentments without that." Today, with inflation, he is probably pulling in $350,000 annually.

And then there was the late Edward Durell Stone, a beguiling, self-styled plain old Arkansas boy who reached his pinnacle of professional success in the 1960s and early 1970s. I had lunch with him one day in a bachelor penthouse, complete with Filipino houseboys, that he maintained atop his townhouse office on Manhattan's upper east side. I say bachelor penthouse because at the time Stone was being sued for divorce by his second wife; in fact the matron in question had been reported in the newspapers the evening before to be demanding a very large maintenance allowance. She contended that Stone could easily afford it; she held he had made a profit of more than a million dollars from his practice the previous year.

"Is it true, Ed?" I asked him.

"Just about true," he admitted. Then he rubbed his chin reflectively and confided that in reality, his personal net had been closer to two million.

In 1981, a relatively healthy year for the economy, Gyo Obata and George Kassabaum, then the principal partners of HOK, each earned $215,000 in salary. There were 44 other people in the firm who made more than $45,000, including the heads of each of the regional offices, who made between $50,000 and $100,000 and leaders of all the specialties and one consultant. Vice presidents' base salaries ranged from $40,000 to $42,000, those of associates from $28,000 to $30,000; entry-level architectural and engineering employees with some experience earned between $15,000 and $18,000, while students started out at $4.50 an hour. Salaries in the regional offices varied further, depending on local living costs and on competition for personnel from other firms; Washington, Dallas and Houston were especially competitive that year, New York and San Francisco a little less so.

None of these figures included bonuses, however, which can add substantially when business is good; in 1981 it was excellent, and the total bonus pool came to a million and a half dollars, which was divided between 477 staff members, including some secretaries; the bonuses themselves ranged from a few hundred dollars on the lowest level all the way up to the $75,000 awarded to top members of the executive committee.

Almost no architectural offices have broad company retirement or pension plans; it is not an expected part of the profession. Some longtime principals of HOK do, however, have deferred compensation. The firm also offers paid health and life insurance beginning at the associate level, and sponsors a dental plan. Daytime parking spaces are provided for the cars of people ranked as associates and above, the equivalent in St. Louis of $50 per month in parking fees, and a lot more in some other cities. Registration and other professional fees are also paid, and in architecture these are not low. In New York City, for example, individual dues to the AIA, including national, local, and state chapters, presently total $314.00 a year.

The company leases automobiles for the use of each of its offices; the senior principals in all the offices get personal cars. A more unusual perk in the firm used to be "spouse travel." Vice presidents were allowed $1,000 a year toward the expense of bringing a wife or husband along on business trips. "This is an absolutely wonderful policy," commented the manager of the Washington office, following a business trip to Charleston, South Carolina. "I took along my wife and she could roam around the city while I was at clients' meetings. It's a little benefit that makes people feel good about their husbands or wives working for HOK. And when one of our staff is tempted by an offer from a competing firm, at the dinner table that night maybe the question is just bound to be asked, 'Well, what's their policy on spouse travel?' "

One of the first victims of the 1982 recession, however, was spouse travel. Other moves to shave outgo, in addition to layoffs of 13 percent of the staff: most salaries above $48,000 were cut 5 percent; the firm stopped buying first class tickets on the airlines for anyone; a $50 a month gasoline allowance for people with company cars disappeared; most people who left the firm, or retired, were not replaced; even George Hellmuth's palatial old office in the Boatmen's Bank Building was sublet, although he and Dorothy Forrest were found a very comfortable new one on a lower floor.

Surprisingly, the bonus program did not vanish, although it was cut way back. When spouse travel returns to HOK, the corner will truly have been turned.

HOK is a privately owned corporation, so its total worth in dollars is not revealed; every now and then, however, a piece of suggestive information surfaces. This happened in 1979, when George Hellmuth stepped down. Because HOK's bylaws prohibit anyone except active employees from owning stock, Hellmuth turned over his shares, amounting to 27% of the firm's total ownership, and received for them close to $2 million, which was secured by HOK on a long term bank loan.

Perhaps a truer indication of the firm's value, however, came seven years ago when a major steel company, interested in taking on HOK as a subsidiary, offered to buy the firm for $12 million—an offer that the partners declined, with thanks.

CHAPTER TEN

Beyond the Establishment

Although the world at large has been kind to HOK (and so have the worldly corporations), the nation's trend-setters in architecture have been less so.

For example, *Architecture* (formerly named *The AIA Journal*), a first rate professional magazine published in Washington, D.C., once produced an article on HOK's Air and Space Museum. It was a good architectural analysis, with superb color photographs, and it praised the building, yet it ended with a paragraph expressing regret that the late Eero Saarinen, who decades earlier had won a preliminary competition for a design on another site, had not finally carried out the commission.

On the East Coast, particularly in New York City, there is and always has been a strong architectural establishment, whose members give lectures, serve on juries awarding architectural prizes, and publish articles on books evaluating and elucidating architecture. Most recently, post modern classicism was promoted in New York, and before that, post modernism; biases are polished and perfected in the architectural-social interplay of the place. The Museum of Modern Art's exhibits on architecture are influential landmarks. Like Japan, Manhattan, in the matter of architectural ideas at least, is an exporter, and imports only grudgingly.

Why is this true? Maybe because a country's largest city does tend to seize cultural leadership. New York has long been the communications and publishing hub of the nation. Women's fashions are still set in New York, and so are most architectural fashions. The American Institute of Architects' Gold Medal for design most usually has been be-stowed on practicing New York architects. Midwesterner Frank Lloyd Wright was not given this award until he was 82 years old; the West Coast architectural genius Bernard Maybeck had to wait for it until he was 90. Another lesser, but cherished, club prize of the AIA is its "Office of the Year" award, for firms that have demonstrated design ability over a period of at least ten years. It, too, generally goes to a New York architect.

Yet several other cities, starting with Chicago, are more impressive architecturally than New York. Manhattan has some fine and fascinating buildings and a stirring skyline, but its best recent work is for the most part polished rather than powerful, and its standard commercial structures have always been mediocre. In the decades since World War II the avenues have been punished particularly. Park Avenue today is cold and grim, Third Avenue gelid, and Sixth Avenue chaotic, while slim Madison Avenue is being overpowered by blatantly out-of-scale new skyscrapers.

It sometimes seems that what New York does best in architecture is to put the rest of the country's architects on the defensive.

HOK is not the only firm to find the going rough in New York. When Hugh Stubbins of Boston first released sketches and models for the Citicorp Tower on Lexington Avenue, local critics gave him a quite cool shoulder, and their attitude changed only after the building was in place and attracting very admiring attention from the public, a clear architectural favorite over rival Chase Manhattan's modern keep in Wall Street designed by the local SOM office. Still more blatant over the years has been the local architects' disdain for Minoru Yamasaki's World Trade Center in lower Manhattan, a pair of nicely proportioned skyscrapers, rather than a single monster, placed off to one side of what is left of the romantic old Wall Street skyline. But Yamasaki designed it in Detroit.

Establishing a branch office in New York doesn't seem to help the out-of-town architects very much. One of the many Manhattan buildings in recent years for which HOK New York made the client's final short list was the 38 story AT&T office building now being completed on Madison Avenue at 56th Street. There Gyo Obata went up against two other finalists for the commission, Kevin Roche of Kevin Roche and John Dinkeloo, Hamden, Connecticut, and Philip Johnson, of Philip Johnson and John Burgee, Park Avenue. The three architects were brought together one Manhattan morning to present, in turn, their qualifications before the AT&T high officers, and Obata recalls: "I went into that room and right away I knew I didn't have the job. They were not listening at all."

Johnson won out. At a party several weeks later, Kevin Roche, a wry man, encountered someone from HOK and remarked, "There was no way either Gyo or I could have got that job. They were sure to select a New York architect."

"But we *are* a New York architect," protested the HOK man.

Roche smiled.

The next big AT&T job that came up, however, in New Jersey, was awarded to HOK.

The world will always need more than one kind of fine architecture. In Washington, D.C., on opposite sides of the Federal Mall, two different kinds stand confronting each other, one statuesque in style, the other functional. The first is architect I. M. Pei's new East Wing of the National Art Gallery. The second is Gyo Obata's aviary of retired airplanes, the National Air and Space Museum.

Pei's gallery has probably received more atten-

tion from the press than any other single American building of the decade past, and it fully deserves the praise. A classic modern structure, exquisitely built and most sophisticated in its complex geometry, it encloses some spectacularly staged spaces, most notably its central reception room. Normal museum traffic wanders in under a low ceiling and suddenly is stunned by that enormous skylit room; then, to reach the upstairs galleries, the public treads respectfully up a long marble staircase before reaching the escalators that carry them the rest of the way.

The grand central room is what the building is really about, and is a magnificent place for a party. But it takes a really big party to bring it to life. More importantly, the room outscales and overpowers any work of art that has yet been displayed in it, including the very large Calder dangling from the intricate skylight.

Pei's East Wing building was paid for by Paul Mellon, a famous patron of art, horses, Yale and architecture, and it is reputed to have cost him close to $100 million. The nation is lucky to have it, and knows it. Yet the old neoclassic wing of the original National Gallery works better as a gallery.

In contrast, across the green is Obata's Air and Space Museum. Rectangular in shape, little more complicated in its mass than an airplane hangar, it is enclosed in straight, plain panels of marble and tinted glass. Like the National Gallery's East wing it is huge, but its presence is very quiet. It is friendly, rather than imposing.

And it works perfectly. It is the most heavily trafficked museum in the world, with as many as 50,000 visitors in the building at one time. Yet the crowds are neither uncomfortable nor overawed as they move on two levels through the three interlinked galleries, looking about them at the displays. The building stands back, granting full center stage to the airplanes, rockets and missiles it was designed to house.

Congress, rather than a private benefactor, paid

for the Air and Space Museum, first authorizing $40 million in 1966, and adhering to that appropriation when the project went forward in 1972, although building costs by that time had almost doubled in the District of Columbia. When the Museum opened in 1976, the Washington *Post* ran an editorial expressing delight that a federal building of such size, for the first time in the memory of the oldest editorial writer, had been finished on time and below budget.

To take a more thorough architectural measure of Obata and his HOK designers, it is necessary to travel a bit, perhaps first heading southwest for a look at the shopping Galleria in Dallas. The great steel arches that support the large central roof have a characterful clout reminiscent of the brawny legs of the Eiffel Tower. The new, buried convention center in San Francisco conveys the same kind of power, in prestressed concrete.

Also in San Francisco is an HOK building group completed in 1981 that may well be the firm's best work yet, for reasons that call for a short digression concerning the site.

Over the years, as the city of San Francisco grew from a small seaport into the prosperous commercial center it is today, a persistent environmental problem has been to preserve the charm that has attracted people to this city ever since gold, the original lure, gave out back in the California hills. That charm is of major economic importance, measurable in the hundreds of millions of dollars spent annually in San Francisco by tourists from the U.S., Europe, and the Orient.

But because San Francisco is a very small city geographically, its builders have often been hard pressed to find sites. First they filled in 20 percent of the big bay. Then in the 1950s they began turning to the opposite kind of site-finding, pushing upward into skyscrapers. The bright new towers and slabs are exhilarating to see from the commuters' ferry, but ashore the dense shadows they throw on the narrow streets are confining and confusing, despite the *brio* of some of the architecture. Worst of all, the clump of skyscrapers packed into that downhill district competes with the city's hillsides, which are still largely residential, and commits the egregious sin of blocking much of their Bay view.

San Franciscans so cherish their city that the skyscrapers became a political issue. In the 1960s the municipal electorate almost passed a law prohibiting the future construction of buildings higher than six stories, and many areas, especially the Bay front, have been put under protective zoning, with strict height limitations imposed to avoid repeating the architectural mistakes of the financial district.

With this background in mind, consider the client who came to HOK in 1975 to get a new corporate headquarters, a big one, three quarters of a million square feet, to be constructed on the San Francisco waterfront: Levi Strauss, the king of blue denim.

This company has a very old name in San Francisco, and might be said to have followed the city's lead in the matter of architectural ups and downs. It was owned by the Haas family up until a decade ago, when it became listed on the New York Stock Exchange and went public, to be recognized as the 160th biggest industrial corporation in the country. As part of the transition from family-owned jeansmaker to stock market heavyweight, Levi moved from its old brick headquarters near the waterfront to a tall, sleek new slab in Embarcadero Center, in the heart of the financial district, thus becoming part of the skyline to the ferry riders. The company found it didn't like its polished new offices, however, and President Walter Haas, Jr., in 1974 asked a team of three developers, who had optioned some real estate adjacent to the waterfront, to rehouse his company's offices there, on a couple of blocks with a view of the Bay. At the time the land was occupied by old warehouses, and since it lay directly below Telegraph Hill, building heights were restricted.

A few weeks later Gyo Obata—with Bill Valentine as his deputy—entered the picture as the designer of what would ultimately become Levi's Plaza, a group of large, low buildings around an open space.

Merely making buildings legally low does not make them good. It would have been easy enough to place the usual highly machined tall office building on its side on this site, bending it to fit the height restrictions, but turning a very impersonal, unyielding face to the city. Instead, Obata broke the project up into three separate buildings (a fourth consists of one of the site's original old warehouses, which has been remodeled by another architect, Gensler & Associates). One of the new buildings is seven stories high, the second is five stories, and the third only four. The two higher buildings have been positioned at the very foot of Telegraph Hill, which becomes precipitously steep as it nears its base, and they are set widely apart so that some old houses on the lower part of the hillside can look out between them to the Bay.

A visitor who walks through the plaza between these buildings emerges into a large, informal, open space designed by landscape architect Lawrence Halprin, with grass, trees, hummocks, paths, and a big splashing fountain. Ahead, just across a public street and slightly to the right, stands the third Levi building, while next to it on the left lies a triangular acre that continues the feeling of the plaza, and which the developer, in a gesture of friendship to the city, has turned into a public park. Here Levi's Plaza ends; beyond lie a few broad warehouses and gleaming San Francisco Bay.

It is difficult to insert 750,000 square feet of office space into an old section of a city without a touch of arrogance, but this has been the achievement here. To merge with the character of the warehouse neighborhood, the HOK designers used a brick veneer panel wall—laid-up brick is no longer legal in San Francisco because of its susceptibility to earthquakes—but used it differently from the brick in the more angular old warehouses; it rounds the corners of the Levi buildings, softening their low shapes. Their bulk has been further diminished by balconies cut back into the long walls, dripping with vines.

Polite as it is to the city, there is nothing smug or bland about Levi's Plaza's architecture. The building shapes are powerfully wrought; the walls edge in and out, giving them shape and scale, and they also step back as they rise. The three buildings differ in shape and height but not in character. Because of the way the land slopes, the building closest to the Bay has a base several feet lower than the other two, resulting in a subtle variation of proportions. This is a mature and controlled piece of urban architecture. People look good in and around these strong but quiet buildings, in the same way they do around Louis Sullivan's humane architecture. They are not diminished by their surroundings, but enlarged.

CHAPTER ELEVEN

Ahead

Architectural practices are created by individuals, but sometimes live on through generations. Will HOK?

Obata and Kassabaum made it clear in 1978 that they intended HOK to survive beyond them when they arranged for the firm to buy up George Hellmuth's stock at the time he stepped down. Allotments of shares were made available for purchase by key employees. A low interest loan program was launched to help some staff members pay for stock and at present there are 46 shareholders. HOK has since granted stock options to 80 employees. Obata possesses the largest number of shares by far. He does not plan to retire until he is 70, a decade from now, and even then he expects to be active in HOK.

Assuming HOK does survive future transitions as well as it has the past ones—and there is ample evidence in the combination of Obata, Graf, Sincoff and their colleagues to indicate that it can—the firm will nevertheless continue to bear not only the names but the strong marks of its originators. Here are some notes on H., O., and K., the founders.

Coda . . .

GEORGE HELLMUTH has been accumulating and embellishing his country place in the Ozarks just about as long as he has HOK. It was in 1952 that he and his wife, Mimi, took title to the first 80 acres, in a valley beside the river; the parcel included an old house, and they paid, as he remembers it, $2,500.

Their holdings now comprise about 2,000 continuous acres of beautifully wooded hills and valleys, with five miles of trout-stocked streams, as well as a dozen lakes and ponds baited with small and big-mouthed bass. Eagles, hawks and buzzards soar in the sky above. Open fields are occupied by the Hellmuths' herd of registered cattle; there is much wild game, and a number of hound dogs and terriers who think they own the place. Hellmuth calls it "comfortable country."

This is the area where, 165 years ago, Hellmuth's great-grandfather settled down, an emigrant from Speyer-on-the-Rhine in Germany. He had first landed in New Orleans, then came up the Mississippi with his wife and young son and two daughters. Both girls perished of cholera during the journey.

Great-grandfather Hellmuth cleared a farm, long since sold off, near the town of St. James. His son, Hellmuth's grandfather, became a manufacturer of iron buckets there, for this was mining country during the 19th century. Though the mines have long since been worked out, the local stone, limonite, is still encrusted with ore, and Hellmuth has accumulated several piles of it on a hillside with a long view, where he plans to build a small memorial chapel. "I've got the site cleared," he says, pointing it out. "I planted those pine trees behind it thirty years ago. It's the prettiest place I know. It's where I'd like to be buried."

Although Hellmuth has always considered his

In the Ozarks, George Hellmuth relaxes at his 2,000 acre retreat on the feeding pier over the trout-breeding pond; below, with some of the charcoal burners on a hilltop; bottom, in one of the cow pastures. Right, Mimi Hellmuth joins her husband and, below, the laird of the evening.

duchy a working farm, he also has entertained many clients there, including Abdullah, the St. Louis prince. "You spend a weekend or a few days with a man," Hellmuth says, "and you get to know him a hell of a lot better than at a meeting. There's a kind of camaraderie that's hard to duplicate in an ordinary way." There have been guests from the office staff, too, over the years and, of course, George and Mimi Hellmuth's five grown children, two of whom are architects, and nine grandchildren.

As one would expect of him, Hellmuth has utilized his property shrewdly. Much of the hilly land one drives through before reaching the inner valley and the lodge is devoted to a managed pine forest, and another portion has been leased to a resort operator, who holds small summer festivals and rents out campsites around one of the lakes. A dozen years ago Hellmuth also began his own charcoal-making operation, now run by four resident Ozark families. His next scheme is to raise ginseng commercially. The herb, which grows wild in the Ozarks, brings a high price when exported to China as an aphrodisiac, and Hellmuth doesn't see why it can't be cultivated in an orderly way, perhaps with guards armed with shotguns to protect it. "The objective," he says, "is to make this place pay for itself indefinitely."

The farm's unofficial name is The Sinks, because two of its larger lakes are distinguished by huge boulders, 40 feet high, with dark tunnel-like fissures at water level, through which feed streams big enough to explore in a canoe, Huck Finn style.

On a recent spring day in his valley, George Hellmuth stood in old country clothes by one of the ponds where he nurtures his trout, and threw food pellets to them, as the muscular fish churned the water. He glanced at the hills rising around him, the big boulder in the bass pond nearby, the cows in a hillside meadow. A trickle of smoke rose from the charcoal burners far off on a hilltop. An osprey flew high overhead. Hellmuth said, "Well, you see how far you can go, and then go as far as you can see."

GYO OBATA was born in a walk-up apartment on Sutter Street in San Francisco in 1923. His father, Chiura Obata, came from a long line of Japanese classical artists; he had emigrated to the U.S. 20 years before Gyo's birth, and eventually became the first Japanese teacher of art at the University of California, in Berkeley.

Gyo's father died, a professor emeritus, in 1975, but his mother Haruko still lives in Berkeley and is also an artist, an expert in classical flower arranging, who at the age of 93 continues her busy teaching and lecturing career, an elegant, merry woman. Mrs. Obata has in her possession a medal presented to Chiura Obata by the Emperor of Japan in 1969 for his help in fostering postwar friendship between Japan and America. Ten years later she, too, received a similar medal from Emperor Hirohito for the same service. Upon request she will show a visitor both medals. "Mine is bigger," she says, her eyes dancing behind her spectacles, and it is.

Gyo, the second of their three children, was a freshman in the architectural school at Berkeley when Japanese planes attacked Pearl Harbor. In the ensuing racial tension, the Obatas decided Gyo should transfer out of California, and he was accepted at Washington University in St. Louis. With his telegram of acceptance in one hand and a suitcase in the other, the young Obata attempted to cross the Bay Bridge to the railroad terminal in San Francisco, but security patrols headed by an Army major turned him back. "Don't worry, Sonny, Uncle Sam will take care of you," he was told.

The next day, following a telephone call to the authorities from the Chancellor of the University (who was a close friend of Chiura's and a fellow member of the Sierra Club), Gyo made it across the bridge and to the station. He says, "I remember taking that train, leaving my family and crossing the Sierra Nevadas, which we considered the East.

"I had a few hours' stop in Denver, and I walked around, and I began to see brick, which I had never seen on the West Coast, which is mostly all wood

or stucco. I thought, 'Gee, the cities are dark and gloomy.'

"And I remember stopping in Kansas City, and more brick, then finally coming into St. Louis in one of those incredible April Midwestern thunderstorms, and it was *all* brick."

In St. Louis, Obata says, there was no feeling of wartime, no nightly blackouts as in San Francisco. The students were friendly. In some confusion, however, the St. Louis draft board classified him 4C, which as he recalls it, meant alien.

The day after Gyo left California, the rest of his family was taken into custody with whatever personal possessions they could carry, and confined with many other Japanese-Americans at a race track. Then after several weeks they were shipped under guard to a desolate internment camp in Provo, Utah. It was here that his father was as-

saulted one night the following spring on his way back to the tarpapered lodgings from the wash house; hit on the head with a pipe, he was blinded, and the authorities gave him permission to travel to St. Louis with his wife as guide to seek treatment. Shortly after their arrival, however, and just before the prescribed surgery, his vision returned. The two senior Obatas were then allowed to remain in St. Louis, where they found work at a local advertising agency as artists.

Gyo Obata graduated from architectural school in three years, then studied under a scholarship at Cranbrook, Eliel Saarinen's architecture and planning school in Michigan. Upon graduation from Cranbrook he was drafted and sent to the Aleutians. Discharged in 1947, he worked three years as a designer for SOM Chicago. Then in 1952, he took a job as Minoru Yamasaki's assistant in Detroit, got to know George Hellmuth, and in due course was recruited to partnership in the new firm of Hellmuth, Obata and Kassabaum. Along the way he got married and fathered three children, one of them a recent graduate of Harvard's school of design who works in the HOK San Francisco office.

One wearing aspect of Obata's career is the hundreds of hours he spends each month aboard airplanes; Susan Sanner, his chief secretary, estimates that last year he flew 150,000 miles. Following a divorce in 1971 from his first wife, he married Nancy McGeehan, who previously had worked for him as his secretary. They were a couple very much on the move for the next dozen years, maintaining residences in New York and San Francisco as well as in St. Louis, and making numerous business trips together, including, over a period of several years, ten expeditions just to the Middle East. That marriage broke up in 1984, and Obata continues his travel alone, married to his profession.

Obata does not drink caffeine in any form, either coffee or tea. He rides a bicycle for exercise regularly, and is a happy gardener. He skis and plays tennis. He usually dines on fish or chicken rather than meat. Indeed, Obata is something of a food faddist; long before their marriage began to fade, his wife used to say, "If Gyo were to read somewhere that eating at a wooden table was unhealthy, he'd stop doing it." This was typical of their comradely, irreverent discourse, while it lasted. For the deck beside their St. Louis suburban house Obata designed an elegant elliptical swimming pool with a white concrete bottom and walls of thin shining stainless steel. "Just like a kitchen sink," Nancy sighed.

Obata has built himself five houses over the years. The first one was small, trim, inexpensive, a young designer's house for a young family. The second was more spacious and predictably modern. This was followed by a vacation house in Michigan, then by the new St. Louis house, completed in 1977, where Obata lives today when he is not on the road. Most of the other homes in the community, an opulent and newish suburb of St. Louis, are plump neo-Colonial-Regency manors; their windows are heavily draped, and they stand at the head of broad lawns whose trees, because they were planted quite recently, are still small. In this neighborhood Obata's is the only modern house, although it is not aggressively so. It stands on a wooded ridge above former farmland on a site that was originally considered unusable by the developer. To reach it, a stream had to be bridged and a steep driveway built. It is a vertical house with five split, interlocking levels, walled outside in tidewater cypress boards bought at a mill in Louisiana, rough sawn, then shipped and tongue-and-grooved in St. Louis. There is no lawn. From the street the Obata house is virtually hidden by the woods, so no curtains are needed over the large glass sections in the walls. The house was completed for an economical $40 a square foot.

Obata's newest home, which is near San Francisco on a 50x120 foot suburban lot, is vertical too. From the workroom on the bottom floor you climb a flight of stairs to two bedrooms, then climb a sec-

ond flight to the top floor, which contains living room, dining room, kitchen, and a large deck suspended out toward the Bay. The house is finished on the outside in stucco.

While he was designing it, Obata spent many hours at the dining room table of his St. Louis home playing the budget game, searching through catalogues for inexpensive but good quality components. When the San Francisco HOK office put the design out for bids the estimates ranged as high as $125 a square foot, but it finally came in at $60 a square foot, very inexpensive for such a steep site. The house stands across the bay from San Francisco on the hills above Oakland; from its deck Obata looks past Oakland's Lake Merit in the foreground, up the peninsula to the skyline and waterfront of San Francisco and beyond that to Golden Gate Bridge stretching away into Marin County, with Mount Tamalpais in the distance. The discreetly modern house fits unostentatiously into its community, the pleasant hill town of Piedmont, where in the years before World War II no one with a Japanese name was allowed to take up residence.

GEORGE KASSABAUM grew up in the small town of Fort Scott in the southeast corner of Kansas; his father was secretary of the local YMCA. He said he decided to be an architect when he was ten years old; he used to pass a Presbyterian church on his way to and from school each day, and he thought it was the most beautiful thing he'd ever seen. Young George went off to Washington University's School of Architecture on the advice of a high school drawing teacher, but he never much liked being a student, and in his senior year he dropped out of college to go to work for Boeing as a draftsman in its Wichita plant. He entered the World War II Air Force, which put him in uniform and then stationed him at a drafting board at Wright Field for the duration. He was quite sure he drew up the bomb rack that was unloaded over Hiroshima by the B-29 Enola Gay, although his superiors at Wright were not saying what the rack was for.

After the war Kassabaum returned to Washington University, graduated in 1947, then stayed on as a teacher of design for five years before venturing out into practice.

George K. retained the edge of Kansas in his voice, as well as in his humor. In describing the 1955 formation of HOK out of elements from the previous firm of Hellmuth, Yamasaki and Leinweber he told a friend: "Hellmuth simply removed one oriental name from the letterhead, Yamasaki, and replaced it with another, Obata; then he took a German name, Leinweber, out, and put another German name, mine, in. And nobody in St. Louis really noticed the difference."

Though Kassabaum as an architectural practitioner always made a point of keeping his hand in—two years before his death, for example, he served as project manager of the $56 million expansion of Duke University's medical center in Durham, North Carolina—most of his office time perforce went to administrative duties. But when he first entered architecture he envisaged a very different kind of life. He neither expected nor aspired to become a managing partner in one of the biggest firms in the country.

Then in the years after joining HOK he gradually began to change his mind about the merits of bigness and smallness in his profession, and by the time he became AIA president in 1968 he was coming out strongly on the side of bigness. This was a stand that caused a stir at some AIA meetings, including one in Arizona in 1965, where the audience consisted mainly of architects from small firms.

"It used to be that the significant work was done in the small office, and the large firms were plan factories," Kassabaum told the assembled practitioners. "Today we have reached the point where the reverse is almost true. Only if we look at architecture by candlelight does the warm glow of sentiment and nostalgia soften the hard realities of the fact that the day of the small office is dead, and the big office is the one that can supply all of the services.''

Outside the office, for Kassabaum, there were always countless collateral community chores to attend to. He served on the boards of both Washington University and the St. Louis Symphony, among others. When a committee in St. Louis needed help, even in such a homely project as arranging for seating installations at the July 4th fireworks display in the river-front park, they called George K. (''Well, he's an architect, isn't he?'') and he obliged.

He fathered three children, all of them grown now, and one an architect. He played a little tennis and golf. He gardened and raked leaves in the yard of the modern house he designed himself out in the country club district. He and his wife Marjory belonged to three of these clubs, although he grumbled that it was too many. They had friends in all of them, however, and did not want to offend by resigning from any. His death left a large hole in the St. Louis communal fabric. Charitable bequests in his will included, among others, $100,000 to Washington University's school of architecture (and another $100,000, unrestricted, to the University), $10,000 to the national American Institute of Architects, and $15,000 to the St. Louis AIA chapter.

Of George K.'s numerous community involvements, George Hellmuth, smiling, says, ''He was the only real social success the firm has had.'' Then he added, ''But he was an architect's architect.''

A few weeks before he died so suddenly, the architect's architect said, about HOK and his own career in it, ''There's a tremendous personal satisfaction that comes from looking back at a building you were part of 25 years ago. It has influenced people—people have enjoyed it, lived in it, worked in it, maybe gotten well in it. And there it stands. It's one thing that architects have, that not too many other people do.''

The Work of HOK

Corporate Headquarters

< *Galleria in Dallas, Texas*

LEVI'S PLAZA
San Francisco, California

Recumbent at the foot of the steep slope of Telegraph Hill, facing the Embarcadero and the Bay beyond, the large (750,000 square feet) business quarters of the Levi Strauss Corporation lie in modest contrast to the bristling skyline of San Francisco's financial district several blocks away. Levi's creates a relaxed urban episode architecturally, another of San Francisco's pleasant places. Pedestrians wander through, or linger for lunch. The emphasis is on horizontals, and the scale humane: the biggest building is but seven stories tall. Balconies bedeck the stepped-back upper offices, dripping with vines. The prefabricated wall panels and columns turn comfortably curved corners. The buildings are strong in shape but unostentatious. Further credits, page 98.

Levi's designer, Obata, had once lived on the steep slope of the hill above, so he knew the architectural nuances of the old brick warehouse district below and was determined not to violate its sprawling ways. Yet the office space he shaped works as efficiently as any commercial skyscraper, and was built within a developer's budget. The triangular park in the sketch below is maintained for the public by the owners. Some of the balconies of the buildings extend executives' offices, the rest employees' lounges.

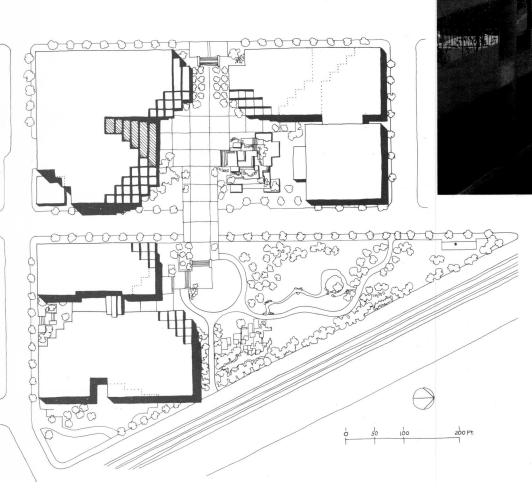

0   50   100   200 Ft.

A fervent fountain by landscape architect Lawrence Halprin provides an amiable site for eating a box lunch, perhaps one to be supplied by one of the various restaurants on the ground floor: Italian, Japanese, seafood, and American bar-and-grill style. The main building is entered by way of a glazed atrium. Interior offices overlooking this entrance have views through the glass roof to San Francisco Bay beyond.

Levi's is constructed on a steel frame with panels of precast concrete studded with inset bricks (conventional brick walls are now prohibited in San Francisco because of earthquake precautions). The steel, where exposed, is painted denim blue.

HOK OFFICE
San Francisco, California

Within three blocks of the Levi
Strauss site HOK established its own
offices on two top floors of an ancient
warehouse, installing skylights and
a private stairway, and renewing
finishes by sandblasting the brawny
timbers and aged brick walls. The
ceilings, wearing exposed ductwork,
are as tall as 25 feet.

MOBIL OIL CORPORATION

U.S. Marketing and Refining Division
Fairfax, Virginia

On 130 acres of wooded land south of Washington, D.C., Mobil wanted an office building of more than 1.3 million square feet, but gave strict orders to the architect to preserve as much of the forest as possible. The gleaming building HOK designed occupies just 24 acres and, further, to keep the upstaging of nature to a minimum, provides underground parking for the 1,100 employees' cars. The structure itself is not at all woodsy, but knife-edged. The spandrel panels of the office wings are duranodic aluminum; the glass is tinted bronze, with silver reflective coating on the inner surface. At the base, and covering the parking garage, is granite. These walls change character continuously with the coloring of the sky and foliage. Mobil's circular towers contain services: elevators, toilets, duct risers, fire stairways. Each of the eight floors has 50,000 square feet of office space in two chunks of 25,000 square feet. Connected with the offices by the bridge of an elevated enclosed walkway over the entrance boulevard is a two story building for large meetings and service of food. Further credits, page 98.

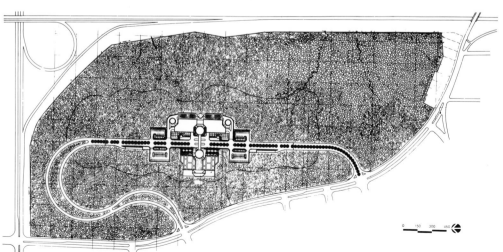

To save energy, Mobil's walls are heavily insulated, with double glazing, and solar collectors sit atop the roof. In addition, buried beneath the building, is a half million gallon water storage tank. This pool provides heating in winter, while in summer the water is chilled during the night at off-peak electrical rates, then used for air-conditioning by day. The building is designed in linear fashion to permit easy expansion.

Art, selected by Mobil consultants Chermayeff and Geismar, gives dash to all the public spaces within the spidery steel framing. Says Obata, "Sometimes sculpture becomes nothing in a building, but if you really study it and place it just right. . . ."

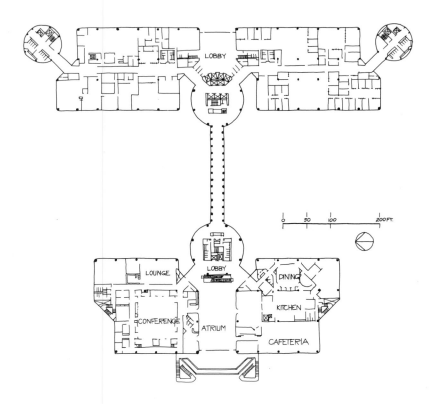

IBM ADVANCED SYSTEMS DEVELOPMENT LABORATORY

Los Gatos, California

The client required an advanced research station for a group of its scientists and technicians, to be sited in a rural valley. To keep the richness of the northern California landscape intact, and to get the building past the zoning board, the architects proposed using rough-sawn redwood (with an extensive sprinkler system). HOK also broke the space of the structure into clusters of offices surrounding major laboratories, keeping the total project from seeming overbearing. Every office views the mountains or an inner landscaped yard. Further credits, page 98.

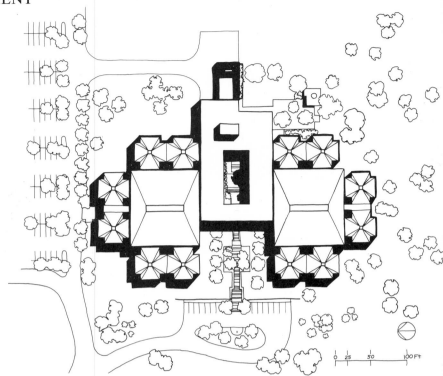

83

E. R. SQUIBB & SONS, INC. HEADQUARTERS

Lawrenceville, New Jersey

Honored as "laboratory of the year" by Industrial Research Magazine, this sizable (about 700,000 square feet) structure houses the multinational client's worldwide administrative and marketing personnel as well as its main research arms: organic chemistry, biochemistry, and pharmacology. The lab is one of many that have sought quiet country settings. Squibb purchased a 273 acre site for it in a largely residential area directly south of Princeton University and faced the usual suspicious resistance from its potential neigh-

bors. This was overcome by considerate site planning and architecture. HOK is now designing an addition to the building. The structural materials are rich: limestone, brick, and bronzed glass, and the shapes are low, long, and unobtrusive for such a large building. The architect created a lake beside the lab. As shown in the photograph above, the platform-like protrusion toward the water contains an employee lunch room virtually at water level. Further credits, page 98.

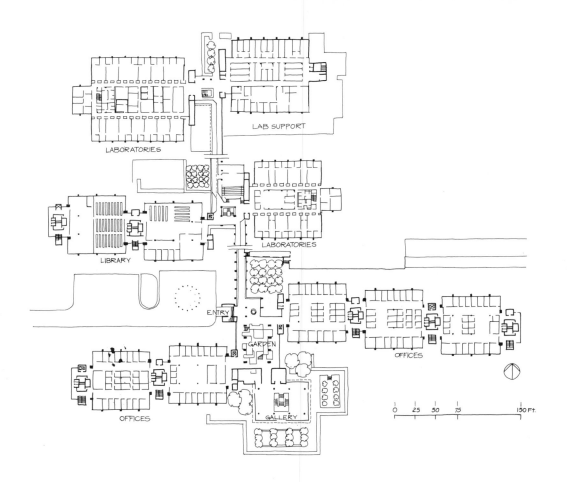

LABORATORIES

LAB SUPPORT

LABORATORIES

LIBRARY

ENTRY

GARDEN

OFFICES

OFFICES

GALLERY

0 25 50 75 150 Ft.

The sweep of the Squibb laboratory is evident in the plan diagram across the page and the aerial photograph below it. But the building is divided into so many components that it is nowhere overpowering seen at ground level. An architectural spine connects all these parts, and itself leads to the lakeside dining room on one end and to training areas at the other end.

The spectacular space across the page is Squibb's entry hall, a lofty room filled with trees, flowers, and the refreshing sound of running water. Shown left is the reception desk; below, right, a typical administrative office, and the dining room on the lake.

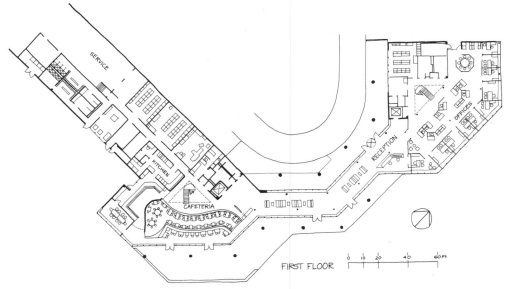

FIRST FLOOR

0 10 20   40   60 Ft

ECHLIN MANUFACTURING COMPANY
Branford, Connecticut

Headquarters for a manufacturer of auto parts, this architectural essay in horizontals is set directly on the rocky Connecticut shore of Long Island Sound and makes the most of its site. Only three stories high, it is folded in plan as it follows the shoreline. Rooms such as the employees' dining room and lounge on the ground floor have generous terraces outside. Most of the private executive offices above also have water views, as do some of the general offices. Those that face inland do not fare badly for view either, overlooking tranquil lawns. Two skylighted atriums with stairways penetrate the full three stories. There are elevators too, but most of the staff seem to prefer walking up and down. The building is finished in pink granite from a local quarry. Further credits, page 98.

MCAUTO COMPUTER CENTER McDONNELL DOUGLAS AUTOMATION COMPANY

St. Louis, Missouri

The aircraft company, actually a diverse conglomerate, wanted an appropriate space-age building for its fastest growing subsidiary, MCAUTO computer services, and wanted it fast. Just two years after HOK's scale model had been approved by the client's board of directors, MCAUTO moved into this huge shell, designed to house one of the most complete collections of wizard electronic machines in the country.

The building's five wings comprise 1.06 million square feet of floor space. The largest block shelters the eerie computer rooms, with row on row of antiseptic high tech contrivances neatly lined up, as well as an energy center to fuel their operation (including several backup electrical sources). Beside the computer rooms are support facilities, then a core, with the entrance, and five sprouts of office space. Further credits, page 98.

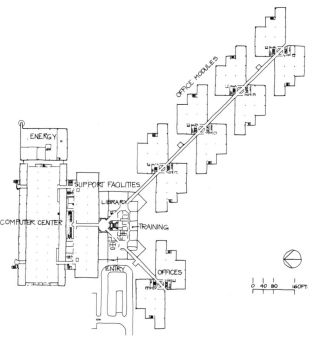

MCAUTO is a simple, gleaming
building, sheathed in a slim, two inch
thick aluminum skin held on a steel
frame. But its innards, especially the
electrical and mechanical services,
are both heavy and complicated. For
example, within the hollow floor
under just one of the computer
rooms, run ten miles of wiring. The
computers produce so much heat
when operating that they could warm
the whole complex four times over
on St. Louis's coldest day.

95

Within the computer center HOK specified vivid colors and emphatic geometrical patternings in a continuation of the abstract character of the exterior architecture. Above is a photograph of the central waiting room; left, the inside of a tube-like corridor linking two wings; below, human thinkers taking nourishment in their lunch room; right, programmers traveling to their stations by escalators.

Further Credits

LEVI'S PLAZA
Client: Levi Strauss & Company
   Peter E. Haas, Chairman of the Board
Developer: Jim Joseph, Gerson Bakar, Al Wilsey together
   with The Equitable Life Insurance Company
HOK Project Team: Gyo Obata, William Valentine,
   Robert E. Stauder, Robert L. Canfield, Ted Davalos,
   James E. Keller, Roger Klemm
Structural Engineer: Cygna Consulting Engineers
Mechanical Engineer: Vann Engineering
Electrical Engineer: The Engineering Enterprise
Soils Engineer: Dames & Moore

HOK OFFICE
Client: Hellmuth, Obata & Kassabaum, Inc.
HOK Project Team: Gyo Obata, William Valentine,
   Roslyn Singer Brandt, Bradley James Hill

MOBIL OIL CORPORATION
Client: Mobil Oil Corporation
   Rawleigh Warner, Jr., Chairman of the Board
HOK Project Team: Gyo Obata, Jerome J. Sincoff,
   James R. Henrekin, Frank Clements, Robert A. Hill,
   Terry Mattison, William Harris, Ken Hanser
Structural Engineer: GCE International, Inc.
Mechanical/Electrical Engineer: HOK Engineers

IBM ADVANCED SYSTEMS DEVELOPMENT LABORATORY
Client: International Business Machines Corporation
HOK Project Team: Gyo Obata, Jerome J. Sincoff,
   James R. Henrekin
Structural Engineer: Gilbert, Forsberg, Diekman & Schmidt
Mechanical Engineer: Harold B. Brehm

E. R. SQUIBB & SONS, INC.
Client: E. R. Squibb & Sons, Inc.
HOK Project Team: Gyo Obata, Jerome J. Sincoff, George Hagee,
   David Suttle, Mike Tatum, Dennis Cassani,
   Charles P. Reay
Structural Engineer: LeMessurier Associates/SCI
Mechanical/Electrical Engineer: Joseph R. Loring & Associates
Laboratory Consultant: Earl Walls Associates

ECHLIN MANUFACTURING COMPANY
Client: Echlin Manufacturing Company
HOK Project Team: Gyo Obata, Harry Culpen, Paul Scovill,
   Roslyn Singer Brandt, Chuck Tewfik
Structural Engineer: Gillum Consulting Engineers, P.C.
   (formerly Gillum-Colaco)
Mechanical/Electrical Engineer: Edwards & Zuck

MCAUTO COMPUTER CENTER
Client: McDonnell Douglas Automation Company
HOK Project Team: Gyo Obata, Peter Hoyt, Robert E. Barr,
   Lou Gogue, David Suttle, Robert A. Jones,
   Charles P. Reay
Structural Engineer: GCE International, Inc.
Mechanical/Electrical Engineer: William Tao & Associates, Inc.

Office Buildings

BOATMEN'S TOWER

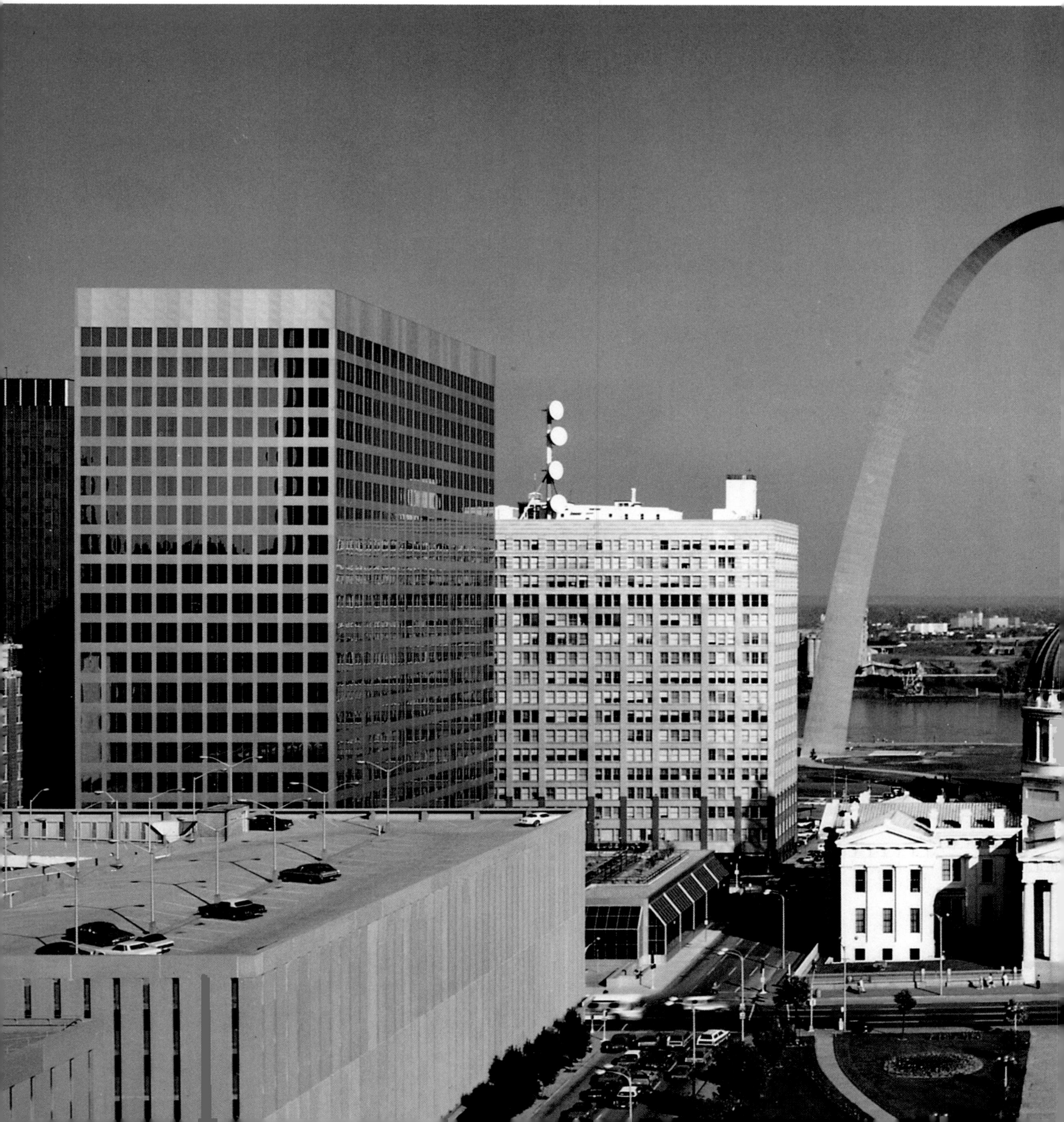

BOATMEN'S TOWER
St. Louis, Missouri

The oldest bank west of the Mississippi is now officed in a 22 story building faced with aluminum and reflective glass. The structure has a uniquely modern banking room on the street level and other tenants on the upper floors, including the St. Louis office of HOK. It is neighbor to the old Federal Courthouse, but does not crowd it, reaching out toward it only at ground level. The banking room shares the tower's entrance lobby and has no partitions except for a bower of trees in the center of the large room. Further credits, page 124.

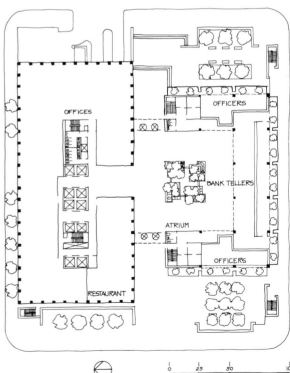

EQUITABLE BUILDING
St. Louis, Missouri

Like the Boatmen's Tower, the tall
bulk of this office building was set
politely back from the old courthouse. Equitable's glittering mirror
wall reflects the historic structure.
The first floor of Equitable, on the
courthouse side of the building,
houses retail space and a swank restaurant and bar (facing page). Equitable, at 21 stories, is a twin in height
to Boatmen's, but was built before
the bank tower, one of the early signs
of a resurgence currently in full
swing in the St. Louis downtown.
Further credits, page 124.

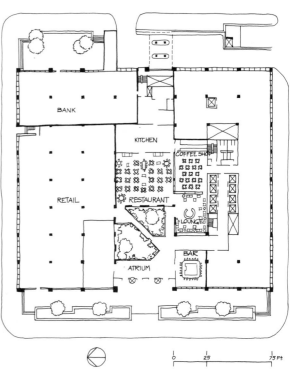

ANTHONY'S RESTAURANT

The bar draws daylight through a full length glass wall fronting the building's sculpture court. In contrast, the restaurant occupies interior space with no windows at all. But in both electric lighting is carefully plotted for elegance. The goblets and glasses on glass shelves in the center of the bar are edged with incandescent light. The restaurant room is dramatized by brass fixtures hanging from the high, dark ceiling, enhancing both food and diners.

RALSTON PURINA WORLD HEADQUARTERS
St. Louis, Missouri

The top 12 stories of this 15 floor concrete shaft, international headquarters for the food products company, contain simple, easy-to-partition loft space. The bottom three floors are devoted to a multi-level indoor garden room and exhibition space with full grown semi-tropical trees, and penetrate below grade for a dining area. Obata deliberately shaped the building to stress the verticality of a grain elevator as a symbol of the client's basic business. Further credits, page 124.

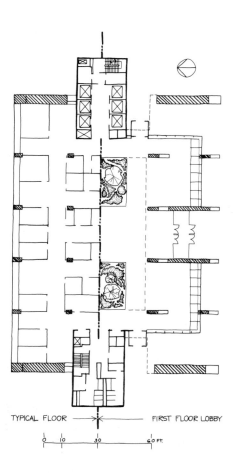

TYPICAL FLOOR ⟶ ⟵ FIRST FLOOR LOBBY

0 10   30   60 FT.

INTERFIRST TWO BUILDING
Dallas, Texas

With 1.8 million square feet of rental
office space, this building was Dallas's tallest when it was completed in
1974: 56 stories, plus a concourse
level below grade connecting with
neighboring downtown buildings.
The structure's reflective silver glass,
a half million square feet of it, trans-
mits only 50 percent of the solar energy received. At night, the cross
bracing wears bright lights. Further
credits, page 124.

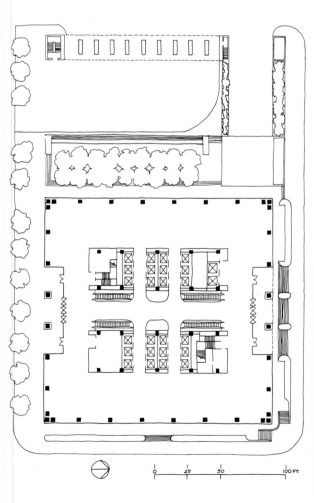

Indoors, the InterFirst Two Building makes no attempt to hide the bracing of its functional frame, instead using it as sculpture. There are two elevator entrances, one from the ground level lobby, shown across page with its sculpture by Charles Perry, the other from the concourse level directly below. The elevators themselves are two-story conveyances, which save considerable space.

FLAGSHIP CENTER
Miami, Florida

Flagship's sleekness against the semi-tropical sky is the result of the combination of the brushed stainless steel wall panels with windows of reflective solar glass impregnated with silver particles. The principal tenant is the Flagship Bank Corporation, whose symbol appears high on the facade. The windows are two heights, short to the sunny side, long to the shade. The sculpture out front is a stabile by Alexander Calder. A second HOK tower is under construction alongside for the developer owning this one, the Nasher Company. Further credits, page 124.

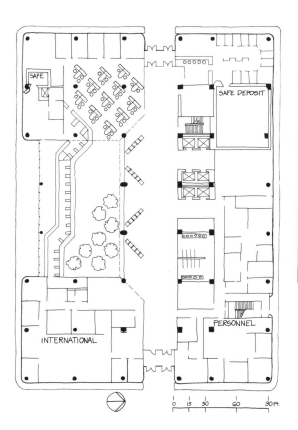

Inside Flagship is a banking room 45 feet tall, resplendent with banners commissioned by HOK. Glass walled on one side, this great room also has a grove of trees growing indoors in air conditioned comfort. Just at the level of the treetops is a gallery with a spacious lounge for the bank's employees. Offices on some of the other floors also look down upon the lofty space.

ARCO MARRIOTT TOWER and PETRO LEWIS BUILDING
Denver, Colorado

Here two structures really add up to three: two office buildings and a hotel. The first 19 floors of the bronze glass walled edifice are a Marriott Inn; above that the structure broadens to become an office building for the Atlantic Richfield Company. Sharing the landscaped plaza at sidewalk level is a second building erected for the Petro Lewis Company. The textures of the two buildings are in contrast. Arco is glazed with thermally reflective mirror glass; Petro Lewis wears a wall of mat finish precast concrete. Placing the narrower hotel atop the office building would have been more economical in cost, but Denver's office workers cherish the view of their mountains from their windows. Further credits, page 124.

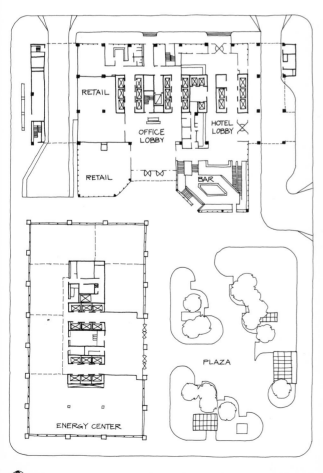

ONE OXFORD CENTRE
Pittsburgh, Pennsylvania

Ultimately to be developed into a
commercial complex occupying six
full city blocks in downtown Pittsburgh (drawing, below) this long-
range project has begun with a strik-
ing office building 46 stories high, its
base consisting of a five-level urban
shopping place and a 900-car parking
garage. Total space enclosed: 1.3
million square feet. In shape, One
Oxford Centre is four structural
shafts around a central axis. The
faceted character of the building is
emphasized by the cladding of the
wall: reflecting glass and silver-gray
aluminum. Further credits, page 124.

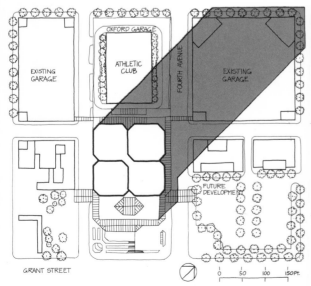

118

The architect says he sought in the character of One Oxford Centre "a building that would appear light and airy despite its strong scale, and glisten in the sunlight." It does the same in the haze, as it shoots up behind one of Pittsburgh's handsome old bridges. The clear span floors of the office tower are shown in plan, below.

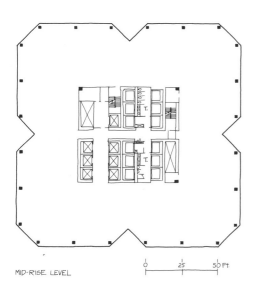

MID-RISE LEVEL

0   25   50 Ft.

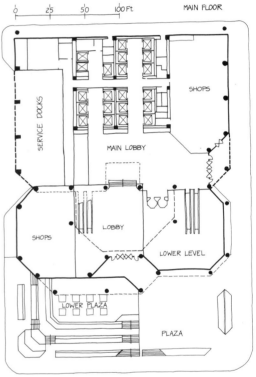

0   25   50   100 Ft.   MAIN FLOOR

SERVICE DOCKS

SHOPS

MAIN LOBBY

SHOPS

LOBBY

LOWER LEVEL

LOWER PLAZA

PLAZA

The skyscraper's seeming simplicity is belied by the sophisticated layout of its lower floors. Five retailing levels climb in galleries up the sides of a tall atrium under a broad skylight. Tenants of the galleries include specialty retail stores, restaurants, and clubs, but because of their placement they do not dominate the office lobby. Escalators move the customers up the retailing cliff, and there is also a pair of glass-walled elevators for shoppers, shown in the photograph above, right, but totally separate from the dignified granite are stainless steel clad elevator banks that convey office workers.

Further Credits

BOATMEN'S TOWER
Client: The Boatmen's National Bank of St. Louis
HOK Project Team: Gyo Obata, Jerome J. Sincoff,
    James R. Henrekin, George Lacson
Structural Engineer: GCE International, Inc.
Mechanical/Electrical Engineer: William Tao & Associates, Inc.

EQUITABLE BUILDING
Client: The Equitable Life Assurance Society of the United States
HOK Project Team: Gyo Obata, Chih Chen Jen, Robert E. Stauder
Structural Engineer: Becker, Becker & Pennell, Inc.
Mechanical/Electrical Engineer: William Tao & Associates, Inc.

RALSTON PURINA WORLD HEADQUARTERS
Client: Ralston Purina Company
HOK Project Team: Gyo Obata, Jerome J. Sincoff, Donald Berry
Structural Engineer: LeMessurier Associates/SCI
Mechanical/Electrical Engineer: HOK Engineers

INTERFIRST TWO BUILDING
Client: InterFirst Bank Dallas
HOK Project Team: Gyo Obata, Chih Chen Jen,
    Charles McCameron, Harry Culpen
Associate Architect: Harwood K. Smith & Partners
Structural Engineer: Ellisor & Tanner, Inc.
Mechanical/Electrical Engineer: Blum Consulting Engineers

FLAGSHIP CENTER
Client: Raymond D. Nasher Company
HOK Project Team: Gyo Obata, Larry Sauer, Velpeau E. Hawes,
    Del Shuford, Cheryl Coleman
Structural Engineer: Ellisor & Tanner, Inc.
Mechanical/Electrical Engineer: Brady, Lohrman & Pendleton

ARCO MARRIOTT TOWER and PETRO LEWIS BUILDING
Client: Urban Investment & Development Company
HOK Project Team: Gyo Obata, Jerome J. Sincoff, Richard Tell,
    Chih Chen Jen, James R. Henrekin, Masao Yamada
Structural Engineer: KKBNA
Mechanical/Electrical Engineer: Ralph E. Phillips, Inc.

ONE OXFORD CENTRE
Client: Oxford Development Company and
    The Edward J. DeBartolo Corporation
HOK Project Team: Gyo Obata, Graeme Whitelaw, Harry Culpen,
    Kenneth A. Vogel, Edwin Taylor, Frank Shenton
Structural Engineer: Gillum Consulting Engineers, P.C.
Mechanical/Electrical Engineer: Cosentini Associates

Airports and Public Places

DALLAS/FORT WORTH REGIONAL AIRPORT
Texas

This transportation complex represents Gyo Obata's determination to cut a vast air terminal down to human scale. Another architectural firm had proposed a single enormous structure; instead DFW was broken into a set of smaller terminals curved around parking fields, entered from a central highway stem. To most people the practical measure of an airport for the traveller is how far he or she has to walk to get to the plane. By this measure DFW is humane. Further credits, page 146.

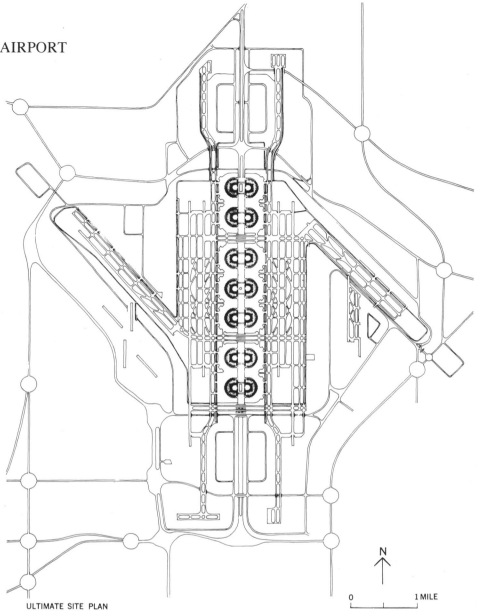

ULTIMATE SITE PLAN

N

0   1 MILE

Before this land became an airport it was occupied by prairie grass, mesquite trees, and a few beef cattle. So far just four of the curved terminal buildings have been finished, but expansion possibilities are almost infinite. The site is 17,550 acres, between the two namesake cities, and can accommodate ten more of what Obata calls "a string of little airports, each with their little parking fields." It is predicted that by the year 2001, when the full complex is expected to be completed, it will be able to handle, annually, the present population of the entire U.S. Transfers between flights and terminals are facilitated by an automated, rail-less trolley that carries people and their luggage. Utility lines to the airport run between the two superhighways, shielded from drivers' view by berms of earth. The whole architectural complex is constructed of precast concrete units.

LUBBOCK INTERNATIONAL AIRPORT, Texas

This is one of the "little airports each with its own parking field" that HOK designed after the Dallas/Fort Worth giant. Lubbock's present comfortable capacity is about 250,000 passengers a year. But it too was designed for growth: the site is 2,500 acres, and the curved terminal could be replicated to multiply capacity by three. All passenger traffic is on the second level of the three-story building; upstairs is office, downstairs, technical areas. Gates are not allocated to individual airlines. HOK's bold graphics, however, such as the banner for gate two, keep passengers aware. Further credits, page 146.

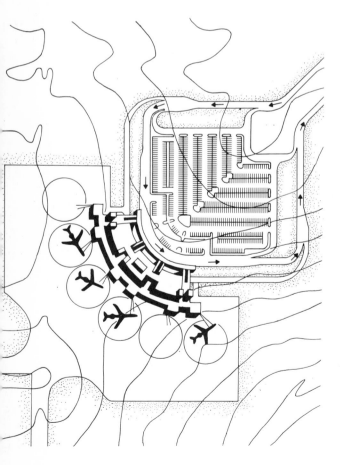

NATIONAL AIR AND SPACE MUSEUM
Washington, D.C.

At its simplest this is an aviary for retired airplanes and space craft. But at the same time it is a gigantic mechanism for moving hordes of people efficiently through the multitude of displays, without confusion. The museum faces north (onto the Washington Federal Mall), allowing the use of large glass panels that show an enticing nostalgic view of the many elderly airplanes and spacecraft hung from brawny tubular steel trusses near the ceiling. Laid out like a shopping mall, the building has two levels of traffic: ground floor and mezzanine. Says the architect, "What I wanted was a museum where you never get lost. You can go quickly in to see one section, or just meander." About a million people a month drop in. Further credits, page 146.

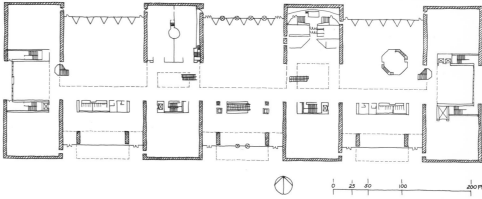

Fine materials used with utmost simplicity, especially the roseate marble from Tennessee, dignify the museum, which stretches a full 685 feet along the grassy mall. With its simple massing, it makes no attempt to upstage its neighbors, other monuments of the nation.

Indoor displays at the Air and Space Museum alternate between the big man-made birds parked on the floor or hovering motionless above, and windowless sections of the building, which contain smaller scale exhibitions and shows. These include a film, ''To Fly,'' a planetarium show, a mockup of a World War I aerodrome behind the Allied front in France, and exhibits on such matters as air traffic control. At present the HOK architects are designing a new restaurant for tired tourists, to be added to the east end of the building at ground level.

THE OLYMPIC CENTER
Lake Placid, New York

Behind the skeletal, geometrically shaped exterior are two skating rinks originally used for the 1980 Olympic games; also dressing rooms, 5,000 permanent theater seats for spectators, and temporary bleacher seating for 3,000 more. The trusses, tied together with smaller members for lateral stiffness, are an expression of the framing that spans 240 feet indoors. Stair towers are walled with glass to give their users vivid glimpses of the Adirondack mountains around the town of Lake Placid. Further credits, page 146.

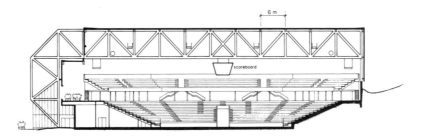

GEORGE R. MOSCONE
CONVENTION CENTER
San Francisco, California

When a bond issue to finance this huge hall went before San Francisco voters, citizens who resented the idea of adding another big building to the city's growing bulk demanded that it be put underground. That was not easy, for the structure is now one of the world's largest exhibit halls without columns. The site is south of Market Street in downtown San Francisco. The tremendous cavern provides 6.3 acres in its main room. Its roof is carried by eight pairs of post-tensioned reinforced concrete arches, each 275 feet in span. Ultimately these muscular concrete supports must also carry a park on the roof with a seven foot depth of earth to nurture trees. Further credits, page 146.

Above ground nothing appears of Moscone except an entrance lobby, conceived as a pavilion in the future park. Walled in glass, it has a roof supported by four tubular steel trusses. Under it is a submerged ballroom with a 25 foot high ceiling supported by steel box girders reminiscent of bridge design. Leading down from the lobby are escalators, stairs, and elevators. The broad well also shunts daylight down to mitigate the claustrophobia of underground.

142

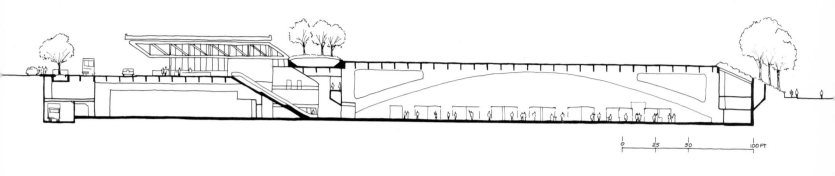

As many as 24,000 people can fit into the main exhibit hall at one time, with more in the other spaces that are a part of the project. A banquet-ballroom, 30,000 square feet in area, has a kitchen capable of preparing 6,000 meals at a time. A combination of metal halide, quartz, halogen, and quartz downlights was installed to provide exhibitors with many different lighting effects. A particularly difficult consequence of placing the exhibit room underground was that it penetrates ten feet below the water table. This required a concrete foundation mat eight and a half feet thick, heavily reinforced, to resist ground water uplift. Just the reinforcing for this massive mat amounted to 8,000 tons of steel. One benefit of the underground approach: the same building constructed above ground would have cost about 25 per cent more to heat and air condition.

DALLAS/FORT WORTH REGIONAL AIRPORT

HOK Project Team: Gyo Obata, J. Tom Bear, Ronald Herbig,
    Charles McCameron

Joint Venture Architect: Brodsky, Hopf & Adler

Associate Architect: Preston M. Geren, Jr.,
    Harrell & Hamilton

Structural Engineer: LeMessurier Associates/SCI,
    Terry Rosenlund & Company

Mechanical/Electrical Engineer: Blum Consulting Engineers,
    Cowan, Love & Jackson, Inc.

LUBBOCK INTERNATIONAL AIRPORT

Client: City of Lubbock, Texas

HOK Project Team: Gyo Obata, James R. Henrekin,
    Herbert Koopman, Donald Berry

Joint Venture Architect/Structural Engineer:
    Whitaker & Hall

Mechanical/Electrical Engineer: HOK Engineers

NATIONAL AIR AND SPACE MUSEUM

Client: The Smithsonian Institution

HOK Project Team: Gyo Obata, Jerome J. Sincoff,
    Chih Chen Jen, Robert Hill, Charles P. Reay

Structural Engineer: LeMessurier Associates/SCI

Mechanical/Electrical Engineer: HOK Engineers

THE OLYMPIC CENTER

Client: 1980 Olympic Organizing Committee

HOK Project Team: Gyo Obata, Harry Culpen, Gerard G. Gilmore,
    Charles P. Reay

Structural Engineer: GCE International, Inc.

Mechanical/Electrical Engineer: Cosentini Associates

GEORGE R. MOSCONE CONVENTION CENTER

Client: City and County of San Francisco

HOK Project Team: Gyo Obata, William Valentine,
    Terril J. Richert, Bradley James Hill,
    Patrick MacLeamy, Jeanne MacLeamy, David Rizzoli,
    Mark Otsea

Associate Architect: Jack Young & Associates

Structural Engineer: T. Y. Lin International

Mechanical Engineer: Hayakawa Associates

Electrical Engineer: Engineering Enterprise

Retail Establishments

THE GALLERIA
Houston, Texas

There are more than a few people in the U.S. who have never heard of the old Milan Galleria in Italy, but know the Houston Galleria intimately. There is a lot to know: department stores, specialty shops, hotels, office buildings, restaurants and entertainment, even an athletic club and an olympic size ice skating rink, and all this a few minutes' drive from inner Houston. The first large specialty store in the Galleria was HOK's design for Neiman-Marcus, but now there are two more large multi-story stores buttressing ends of the complex. In total the Galleria is home to 257 separate retail establishments. Truck deliveries are made through underground concourses; escalators lift the customers into place from underground parking areas. It is a contained merchandising world, where interior traffic seldom wanes. Further credits, page 164.

Stacked around the Galleria's ice
skating rink are three levels of
stores. Above it all, beaming daylight
down, is a skylight 550 feet long,
with double layered glass to filter out
much of the heat of the Texan summer sun before it melts the ice.

Says architect Obata about the Galleria: "Everything feeds on itself. We didn't want a typical suburban shopping mall, but something denser."
He adds, "The design demand is to make the circulation clear and understandable to people who come here."
On the facing page a large glass end wall admits daylight to the central atrium of a balconied office building.

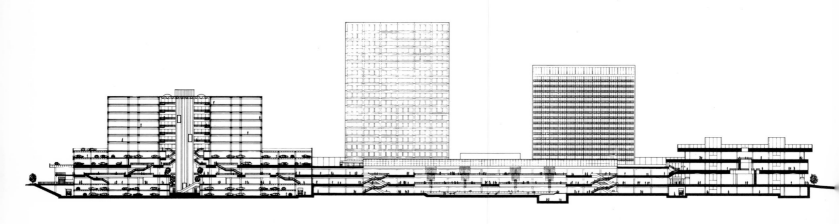

SAKS FIFTH AVENUE
San Francisco

The design of this five story specialty store is rather unique in contemporary merchandising. Whereas most department stores are mere warehouses in appearance above the first floor, Saks has several large windows at various levels, helping it to fit gracefully into this important corner on the Bay City's verdant Union Square. Escalators are so placed that shoppers on any floor must perambulate past the merchandise displays, in order to get the next escalator up. Further credits, page 164.

HULEN MALL
Fort Worth, Texas

The handsome exterior lettering on the canopy of this suburban landmark is a low key announcement of an exciting interior: two levels including 80 varied stores, each level a shopping sidewalk 530 feet long, with department stores at both ends. The spidery exposed steel framing, with clerestories and skylights cut into the trussed roof, and ductwork made into decoration, recalls a botanical garden, and there is plenty of planting too. Further credits, page 164.

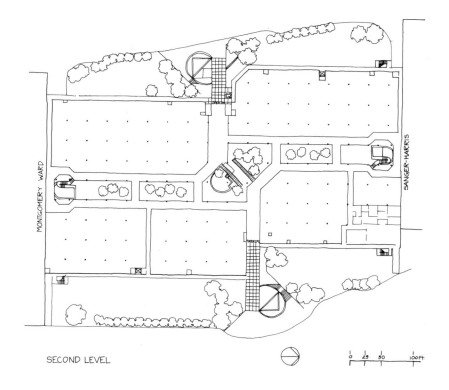

SECOND LEVEL

Grouped around the surge of a tall waterspout on the lower level in Hulen Mall are restaurants. Escalators connect the two levels. Design was done by HOK, complete from mall lettering to engineering, including the installation of an antique clock, clocktower size, refurbished and hung in a big glass case above the interior garden.

GREENWICH SAVINGS BANK
New York City

On Lexington Avenue near Grand Central Station, this small bank occupies a site only 45 feet by 110 feet. Moreover, prior claims on the property, a 15 foot wide truck easement for the loading bay of a hotel next door, further narrowed the effective frontage. HOK solved the problem by placing the tellers on a mezzanine level, with an escalator to carry traffic up to them. The esthetic is stainless steel-*cum*-honed Italian gray granite, red carpeting, and, to magnify the effect, mirror walls. Further credits, page 164.

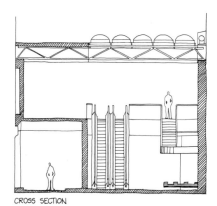

CROSS SECTION

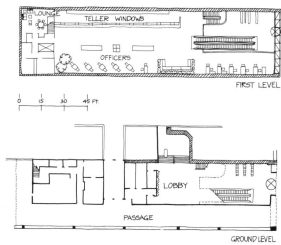

LOUNGE TELLER WINDOWS

OFFICERS

FIRST LEVEL

0   15   30   45 FT.

LOBBY

PASSAGE

GROUND LEVEL

CONNECTICUT POST MALL
Milford, Connecticut

The history of contemporary shopping centers, islands of stores grouped in the middle of seas of parking spaces, long since has evolved into buildings connected by enclosed walkways. HOK was asked to update one of the earlier type, and did it with enough elan to attract a new department store that not only fattened the owners' rent rolls, but provoked merchandising synergy for all the tenants. Prefabricated steel trusses support the roof; continuous strip clerestories flood the mall with daylight. Added were landscaping, banners, and other diversions by HOK's graphics people to make shopping expeditions festive. Further credits, page 164.

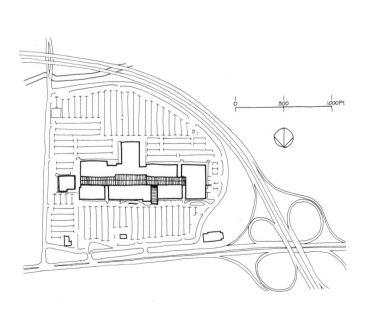

Further Credits

THE GALLERIA (Phase I)
Client: Gerald D. Hines Interests
HOK Architect: Gyo Obata
Associate Architect: Neuhaus & Taylor
Structural Engineer: Ellisor & Tanner, Inc.
Mechanical/Electrical Engineer: J. E. Guerrero

THE GALLERIA (Phase II)
Client: Gerald D. Hines Interests
HOK Project Team: Gyo Obata, David Suttle
Associate Architect: S. I. Morris & Associates
Structural Engineer: Ellisor Engineers, Inc.
Mechanical/Electrical Engineer: Chenault & Brady

SAKS FIFTH AVENUE
HOK Project Team: Gyo Obata, William Valentine, James Fair
Structural Engineer: GKT Engineers
Mechanical/Electrical Engineer: Hayakawa Associates

HULEN MALL
Client: The Rouse Company
HOK Project Team: Gyo Obata, Charles McCameron,
        Donald Lee, Jerry Sparks
Structural Engineer: Charles F. Terry, Inc.
Mechanical Engineer: Broyles & Broyles
Electrical Engineer: Burton Brothers

GREENWICH SAVINGS BANK
HOK Project Team: Gyo Obata, Chih Chen Jen
Structural Engineer: Office of James Ruderman
Mechanical/Electrical Engineer: Jaros, Baum & Bolles

CONNECTICUT POST MALL
Client: The Rouse Company
HOK Project Team: Gyo Obata, Harry Culpen
Structural Engineer: Levien, Deliso & White
Mechanical/Electrical Engineer: Sidney Barbanel

Education and Two Chapels

CECIL H. GREEN GRADUATE LIBRARY
Stanford University,
Palo Alto, California

Campus architectural traditions were observed here. Stanford's older buildings feature red tile roofs and beige walls; so do the wings added to its old library by HOK. The new spaces, however, relieve the formidable scale of the old, and are more comfortable to use. Stacks are in the center of the reading rooms, and a covey of study carrels face outward over the lawns. Primarily a research library for graduate students and faculty, the building has many private spaces, including quiet typing rooms. Further credits, page 184.

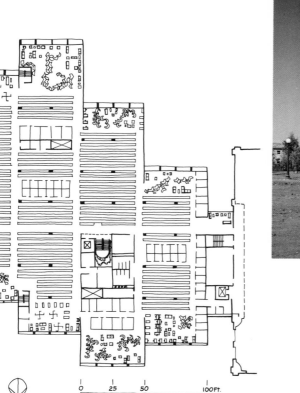

LIBRARY/STUDENT CENTER UNIVERSITY OF WISCONSIN
Parkside Campus, Kenosha, Wisconsin

HOK first did the master planning for eventual development of this campus, a large one enrolling 25,000 students, mostly commuters living at home. Then the firm was asked to design several of the buildings. The largest is a combined library-student center, very important as a mixing place for the commuters. Behind the slotted windows of the facade above are library rooms. On this page are shown two of the generous social rooms. Because of the chill winter climate of Wisconsin, all the buildings were connected in the master plan for comfortable passage. Further credits, page 184.

169

OWEN GRADUATE SCHOOL OF MANAGEMENT
Vanderbilt University, Nashville, Tennessee

Growing from an antique Victorian building, usually called "Old Mechanical" because it was once devoted to the teaching of engineering, Vanderbilt University's new graduate school of management has turned into a much different architectural animal. The new 101,000 square foot structure has a library of 17,000 square feet, a large lecture hall, and numerous classrooms and offices. It also abounds in informal common areas for student relaxation and interaction, including the courtyard formed by the new building. What is modern is properly deferential to what is Romanesque. The new curved inner wall, fully glazed for daylighting, embraces the old campus landmark. Further credits, page 184.

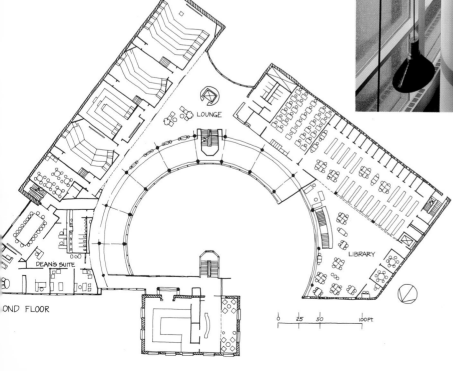

SECOND FLOOR

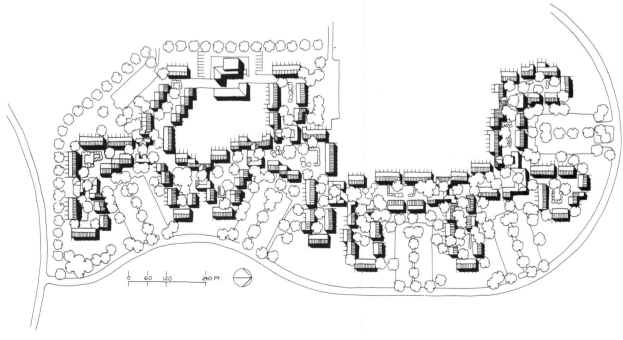

MARRIED STUDENTS' HOUSING
University of Michigan, Ann Arbor

HOK's site planners here devised a
series of contained inner yards for
children to play away from traffic,
while, for easy monitoring, their parents' kitchen windows were all aimed
into these playgrounds. Cars are held
in parking lots outside the juveniles'
zone. The feeling of the 400-unit
complex is homelike, and for economy in construction HOK did not put
the project out to bid to general contractors, instead selecting a smaller
scale housebuilder. Further credits,
page 184.

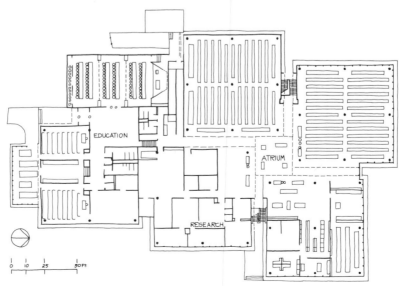

THE JOHN S. LEHMANN BUILDING
Missouri Botanical Garden
St. Louis, Missouri

This building in Shaw's Garden consists of a series of 65 foot by 65 foot modules, with several large skylights pulling daylight down to desk level for botanists working with the many thousand dried plant specimens. The same size modules can easily be added when more space is needed. The material selected for construction was a combination of concrete to echo the existing old house in the background, and reflecting glass to show the greenery twice. Further credits, page 184.

175

RIDGWAY CENTER
Missouri Botanical Garden
St. Louis, Missouri

Under a projecting barrel vault, made of translucent fiberglass in a steel frame, lies the entrance to an education building dedicated to merchant Henry Shaw, who founded this 79 acre garden in 1847. That was just four years before the opening of the Crystal Palace in London, and the new building recalls the spirit of the old. Inside are educational exhibits, a plant shop, research facilities, offices, a restaurant, and an auditorium. As the St. Louis sky lightens and darkens, lighting inside the center is automatically dimmed or raised. At night rows of glittering low voltage lamps outline the exterior. Immense banners of frail fabrics hung inside are printed with enlarged details of various flowers, the work of the HOK graphics people. Further credits, page 184.

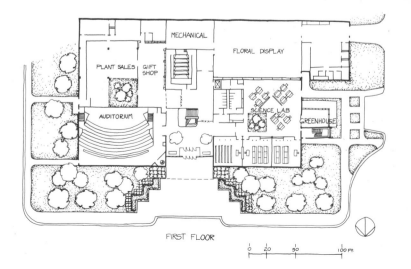

FIRST FLOOR

BARTLETT-BEGICH HIGH SCHOOL
Anchorage, Alaska

Built compactly, with completely enclosed circulation because of cold
winters, this large combined junior-
senior high school nevertheless al-
lows segregation by age group. The
structural system permits flexibility
in room division; even the roofs of
the classrooms have 60 foot spans.
Structural framing is composite, with
steel for the spanning, and stairwells
and utility cores of reinforced concrete to provide lateral resistance
against earthquakes. The gymnasium
seats 1,700. Further credits, page 184.

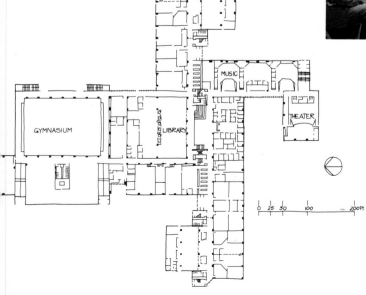

179

BRISTOL PRIMARY SCHOOL
Webster Groves, Missouri

The first public school designed by HOK, and one of the very first commissions won by the then new partnership, was a hint of what was to come. It was fitted carefully into a wooded landscape, had dignity and utility. The classrooms were clustered around a large multipurpose room. Further credits, page 184.

SAINT SYLVESTER CHURCH
Eminence, Missouri

This small, simple church in the Ozarks is constructed of stone from the fields around the town. The congregation did much of the construction itself. Roof beams were hewn from tree trunks. The sheathing of this roof is two-by-fours of local oak.

THE PRIORY CHAPEL
Creve Coeur, Missouri

The HOK partners were asked by the Benedictines to create a small church of contemporary architecture. The sharp thin arches of the shell concrete roof were constructed by a combination of poured-in-place concrete and liquid concrete shot at the mesh reinforcing through hoses; it is the shape of the roofs that makes them strong. Functionally, each arch connotes an individual monk's altar around the periphery. In the center a shell bell tower, with clerestories, completes the evocative daylighting. Further credits, page 184.

182

Further Credits

CECIL H. GREEN GRADUATE LIBRARY
Client: Stanford University
HOK Project Team: Gyo Obata, William Valentine,
    Jeanne MacLeamy, David Rizzoli
Structural Engineer: Gillum, Kacyra, Tandowsky
Mechanical Engineer: Hayakawa Associates
Electrical Engineer: Engineering Enterprise

LIBRARY/STUDENT CENTER
Client: University of Wisconsin
HOK Project Team: Gyo Obata, Herbert Koopman,
    James Henrekin, Robert Barr
Structural Engineer: LeMessurier Associates, Inc.
Mechanical/Electrical Engineer: HOK Engineers

OWEN GRADUATE SCHOOL OF MANAGEMENT
Client: Vanderbilt University
HOK Project Team: Gyo Obata, William Odell, Tad Tucker,
    Thomas Goulden
Structural Engineer: GCE International, Inc.
Mechanical/Electrical Engineer: HOK Engineers

MARRIED STUDENTS' HOUSING
Client: Regents of the University of Michigan
HOK Project Team: Gyo Obata, Robert Edmonds,
    Chester Roemer, James Agne
Structural Engineer: The Engineers Collaborative
Mechanical/Electrical Engineer: HOK Engineers

THE JOHN S. LEHMANN BUILDING
Client: Missouri Botanical Garden
HOK Team: Gyo Obata, Charles McCameron, Charles Danna,
    William Ziervogel, Dean Smith, Charles P. Reay
Structural/Mechanical/Electrical Engineer: HOK Engineers

RIDGWAY CENTER
Client: Missouri Botanical Garden
HOK Project Team: Gyo Obata, Masao Yamada, Charles Danna,
    William Ziervogel, David Suttle, Charles P. Reay
Structural Engineer: GCE International, Inc.
Mechanical/Electrical Engineer: HOK Engineers

BARTLETT-BEGICH HIGH SCHOOL
Client: Anchorage Borough School District
HOK Team: Gyo Obata, William Valentine, Patrick MacLeamy
Structural Engineer: Andersen, Bjornstad, Kane, Arthur, Jacobs
Mechanical/Electrical Engineer: Crews, MacInnes & Hoffman

BRISTOL PRIMARY SCHOOL
Client: Webster Groves School District
HOK Architect: Gyo Obata
Structural Engineer: John P. Nix
Mechanical/Electrical Engineer: Ferris & Hamig

THE PRIORY CHAPEL
Client: Benedictine Preparatory School of St. Mary and St. Louis
HOK Architect: Gyo Obata
Structural Engineer: Paul Weidlinger
Supervising Structural Engineer: John P. Nix
Mechanical/Electrical Engineer: Harold P. Brehm

Medical and Correctional Facilities

MEMORIAL HOSPITAL
Colorado Springs, Colorado

The architectural problem was to renovate and greatly expand an elderly hospital and add a new entrance. As the dining room, overlooked by galleries, indicates, the new design achieved its goals without a sense of stringency. The major addition is a two-level pavilion with a tower rising five floors above it containing 200 new bed spaces for patients in intensive care, along with all necessary diagnostic and treatment facilities. The construction is a reinforced concrete frame clad in brick and reflecting glass. Further credits, page 204.

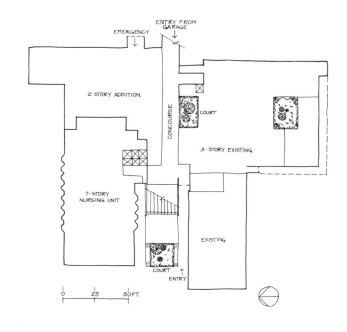

The architects shoehorned the required new spaces into a constricted site by using angular forms. The emergency entrance (above) juts from an otherwise blank wall to avoid confusion. Future expansion, necessary in almost all hospitals, has also been provided for. A new garage has been built on an adjacent site with a frame strong enough to expand vertically for the addition of more medical space above.

188

INCARNATE WORD HOSPITAL
St. Louis, Missouri

A community hospital of medium size that opened its doors about the turn of the century, Incarnate Word had outgrown its old building and had either to move or remodel. It chose the latter course, engaging HOK to develop a master plan for additions and renovations over a period of several years. The first new wing, a 23 bed intensive care unit, combines efficiency with architectural compassion for patients and visitors. A two story skylighted atrium near the entrance (left) constitutes the visitors' waiting room. Beyond, patients' rooms all have two doors, one on a pleasant hallway for visitors to use, the other across the room for fast access by doctors and nurses. Each room is equipped with life support systems that are monitored continuously at central consoles. A chapel and dining room on ground level complete the building. Further credits, page 204.

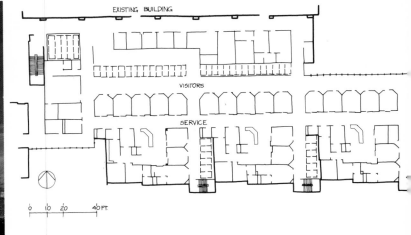

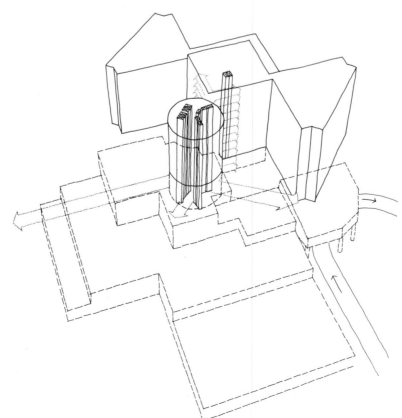

DUKE UNIVERSITY HOSPITAL
Durham, North Carolina

This large addition to an already existing hospital had to be placed 1,200 feet from the parent building group, yet still share clinics and other support services. The solution was rapid transit; shuttle cars run between old and new groups. The central round tower provides vertical circulation and is the meeting point for all horizontal traffic as well. The complexities of adding an immense (750,000 square feet, 616 beds) set of specialized services are suggested by the sketch and overall photograph below. Further credits, page 204.

Among the many advanced technical construction features of the new Duke Hospital are the use of interstitial floor framing, which preserves a layer of space between floors. In this layer of space, among the supporting trusses, are catwalks, so that supply lines and services can be changed or added to without demolishing ceilings or existing mechanical lines. One reason this hospital works so well is that it strictly separates visitors from treatment sections. For instance, the patients' rooms (all singles, no wards) are in a tower by themselves, so that the corridors "aren't thoroughfares to go anywhere else," says Dr. William G. Anlyan, vice president for health affairs at Duke. The interior photographs here show Duke's garden lobby from two levels.

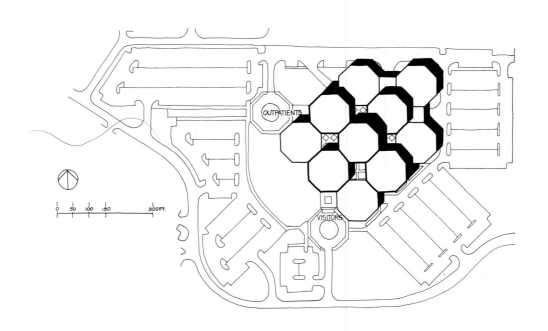

JOHN L. McCLELLAN MEMORIAL VETERANS' HOSPITAL

Little Rock, Arkansas

Though quite a large complex, HOK's Little Rock design is less forbidding than most hospitals and more diverting architecturally, with its sets of windows gazing forth out of square or round fields of blue glazed brick. Located on a site contiguous with the University of Arkansas Medical Center, the hospital provides diagnosis and treatment, with a total of 505 beds for medical, surgical, neurological, and psychiatric patients, and in addition accommodates the needs of a modern university-oriented teaching hospital. Floor area, 750,000 square feet. Further credits, page 204.

197

EAGLE RIVER CORRECTIONAL CENTER
Eagle River, Alaska

There does exist a condensed conventional maximum security wing at this unusual criminal confine near Anchorage, but most of the prison instead emphasizes changing the inmates' patterns of behavior. The architecture provides a relatively informal background, with cedar siding, shed-roofed pleasantness, low proportions, large windows (of security glass), wooden furniture, and retention of trees on the muskeg. More like a campus than a prison, it gives its inmates the choice of participating in extensive counseling and communal living, or not, and most do. The site is 207 acres of forest land near the Chugach Mountains. Further credits, page 204.

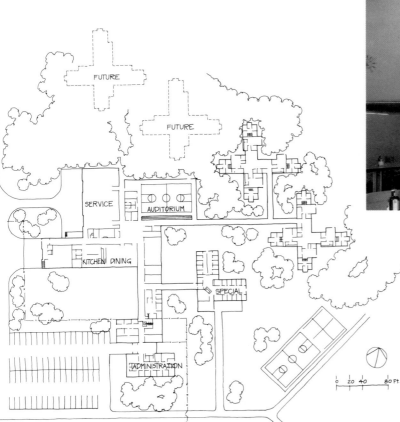

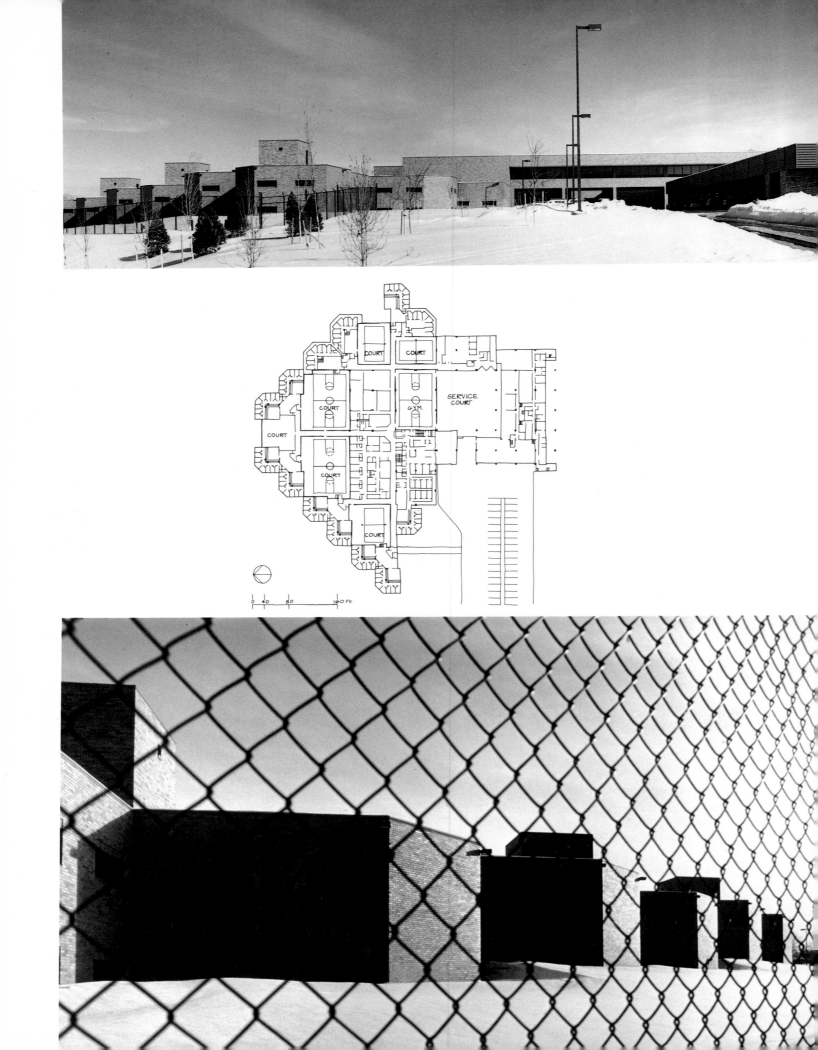

WASHTENAW COUNTY CORRECTIONS CENTER
Ann Arbor, Michigan

The entrance to this predominantly pretrial detention center for 239 arraigned men and women was designed to fit the scale of the largely residential community it inhabits. Living units of eight single occupancy rooms are arranged around a dining room to which meals are delivered from a central kitchen. Each two of these units has a shared day room opening onto an outdoor yard. A larger building contains admission, processing, and booking facilities, a library, classrooms, offices, a staff dining room, and clinics. The fenced site is a sloping 39 acres. Further credits, page 204.

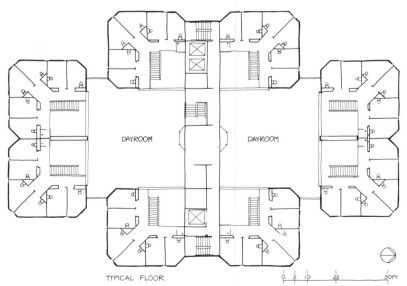

DAYROOM   DAYROOM

TYPICAL FLOOR

BERNALILLO COUNTY DETENTION CENTER
Albuquerque, New Mexico

Urban detention buildings are of necessity compact, and are often ominous in their appearance. This one in New Mexico is formidable but omits all bars from its windows, indoors and out. The exterior openings are long slits in the precast concrete panel walls, too narrow for inmates to wedge through. The barless windows have another advantage; they cost only about half the usual barred version. The plan is also economically compact. Each six cells share a small day room and each thirty a larger room. In a penthouse up top are indoor exercise areas. Further credits, page 204.

MEMORIAL HOSPITAL
HOK Project Team: George Kassabaum, Gyo Obata,
    Charles McCameron, Tad Tucker, John Lesire
Associate Architect: Robert G. Muir & Associates
Structural Engineer: GCE International, Inc.
Mechanical/Electrical Engineer: Rice, Marek, Harral & Holt, Inc.
Hospital Consultant: John B. Warner & Associates

INCARNATE WORD HOSPITAL
HOK Project Team: Gyo Obata, David Suttle, Herbert Koopman,
    Charles P. Reay
Structural Engineer: GCE International, Inc.
Mechanical Engineer: Crawford & Witte
Electrical Engineer: Van & Vierse

DUKE UNIVERSITY HOSPITAL
Client: Duke University
HOK Project Team: George Kassabaum, Gyo Obata, Larry Sauer
    Donald Berry, Robert Hill, Kenneth A. Vogel,
    John Lesire, Bruce Sprenger
Structural Engineer: GCE International, Inc.
Mechanical/Electrical Engineer: Hayakawa Associates

JOHN L. McCLELLAN MEMORIAL VETERANS' HOSPITAL
Client: Veterans Administration
Joint Venture Architects:
    Cromwell Neyland Truemper Levy and Gatchell, Inc.
    Stuck Frier Lane Scott Beisner, Inc.
    Mott Mobley Richter McGowan and Griffin
    Wellborn Hardwick Henderson
HOK Team: Gyo Obata, Donald Berry, George Eisenberger,
    David Gnaegy
Structural Engineer: GCE International, Inc.
    (Formerly Gillum-Colaco of Washington, D.C.)
Mechanical/Electrical Engineer: Syska & Hennessey
Medical Consultant: Leroy Pesch

EAGLE RIVER CORRECTIONAL CENTER
Client: State of Alaska
HOK Project Team: Gyo Obata, William Valentine,
    Patrick MacLeamy
Associate Architect: CCC Architects and Planners
Structural Engineer: Pregnoff, Matheu, Kellam, Beebe
Mechanical Engineer: Hayakawa Associates
Electrical Engineer: Crews, MacInnes, Hoffman

WASHTENAW COUNTY CORRECTIONS CENTER
Client: Washtenaw County Building Authority
Associate Architect: Colvin-Robinson Associates, Inc.
HOK Project Team: Gyo Obata, Bernard Bortnick,
    Chester Roemer, Dale Kostner
Structural Engineer: GCE International, Inc.
Mechanical/Electrical Engineer: HOK Engineers

BERNALILLO COUNTY DETENTION CENTER
Client: New Mexico Department of Corrections and Detention
Associate Architect: Boehning, Protz & Associates
HOK Team: Gyo Obata, Patrick MacLeamy, Frank McCurdy
Structural Engineer: McCornack & Burns
Mechanical/Electrical Engineer: Hayakawa Associates

Projects in Planning and under Construction

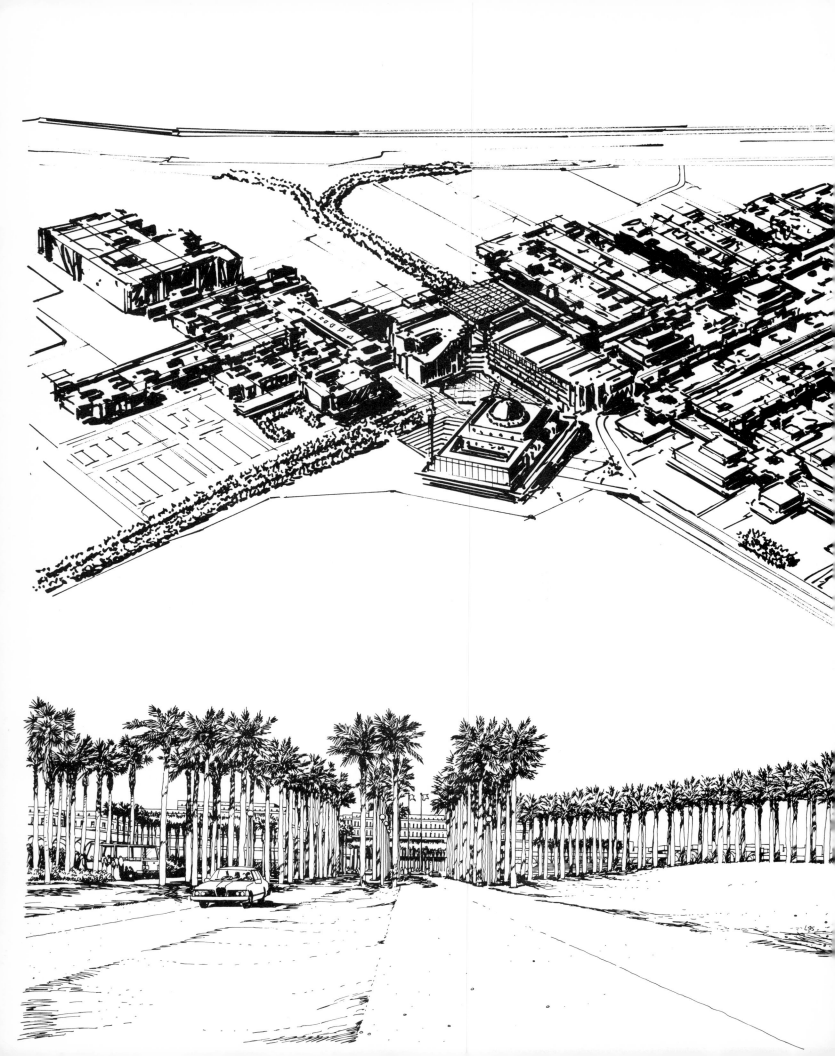

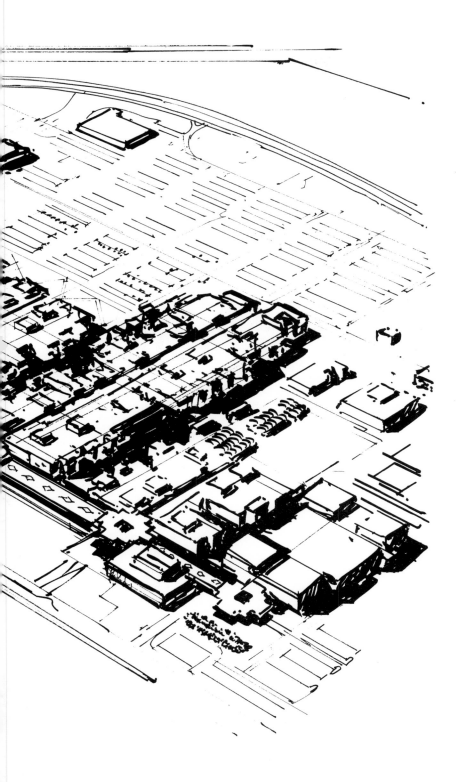

KING SAUD UNIVERSITY
Riyadh, Saudi Arabia

Possibly the largest civil architectural commission of the century so far, this complete-from-scratch university job was won by an international consortium led by HOK. It is well along toward completion. In plan, leading out from a central core of large community buildings, will be three elevated walkways, covered by canopies of concrete arches, which connect to the three general academic areas: medicine, arts, and sciences. Pedestrian traffic is on second floor level; beneath is a service way for utility mains, all of which emanate from a vast central utilities complex. Initial enrollment at the university will be 15,000, and is expected to rise to 20,000 soon. The college of arts alone has 559 classrooms, faculty offices, laboratories, and conference rooms. The college of sciences has 932. But beyond the statistics is Obata's design, a reflection not just of Western technical abilities but Middle Eastern traditions. The architecture is functional modern, based on Arabia's old central Najd style, equally functional. In this style, buildings were constructed close together in order to shade each other from the searing sun; windows were small, inset, and used various shading devices. The ancient building material was light brown unfired mudbrick, smoothed over with mud plaster. The modern university's large precast walls are concrete of the same color. The ceremonial entrance to the university, shown in the lower drawing, will be tree-lined and will terminate at a central plaza containing a mosque. Further credits, page 230.

The insistent need for closure against the fierce sun has not meant that the brilliant Arabic light from the sky will be lost to King Saud University's future students. Alongside a central open plaza, with its pair of splashing fountains, will be a vast landscaped interior courtyard, seven stories high and roofed with a steel frame penetrated by a huge skylight, shown here under construction and in the drawing to the right.

Shading devices used on the walkways are intermittent, providing pedestrians a combination of shadow and bright sky, as shown in the drawing. Before the construction of the university itself was begun, what is thought to be the largest concrete prefabricating factory ever was put up in the desert to manufacture the components of the design, which were then hoisted into place.

KING KHALED INTERNATIONAL AIRPORT
Riyadh, Saudi Arabia

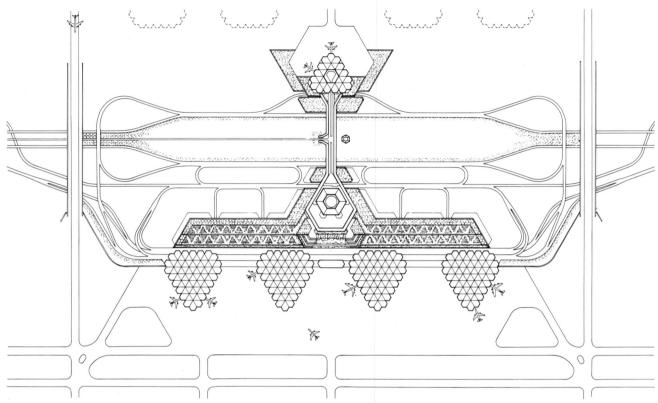

On a 94 square mile site 22 miles north of Riyadh a complex of airport terminals is being completed, to be capable of handling, by the year 2,000, an estimated 15 million passengers per year. Each of the four major public terminals, two international and two domestic, is roofed by 72 triangular steel modules, as shown in the photograph above. The clerestory windows between them are filled with double insulating glass. In the center of the airport is a mosque accommodating 5,000 worshippers indoors, plus another several thousand on its plaza. The mosque in addition serves as a symbol to arriving air passengers from other lands of what this oil-rich country is really about. All interiors will feature gardens with fountains. Jets from one of the fountains are shown in the photograph to the right. The first stage of the airport became operational in late 1983. Further credits, page 230.

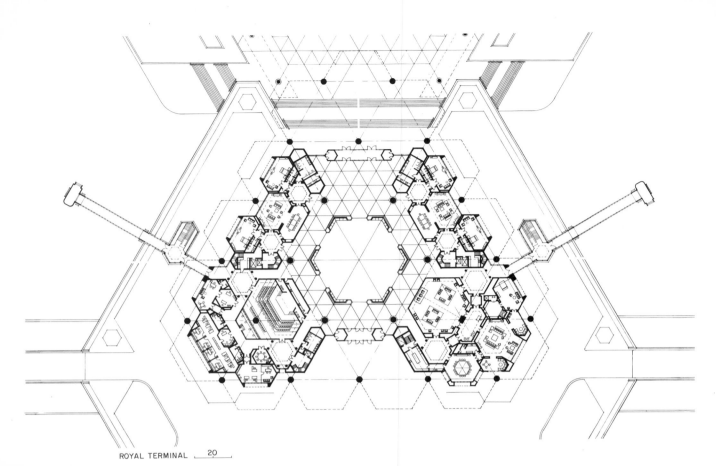

ROYAL TERMINAL ⌐ 20 ⌐

The royal family's richly finished private terminal is smaller than the four public ones but similarly constructed. It is to be used also for ceremonial arrivals of visiting notables. A long mall, flanked by low groves of broadleaf evergreen trees, links it to the mosque.

The airport's mosque will be one of the biggest in Arabia, hexagonal in plan, 170 feet on each side under a mighty steel framed dome, shown under construction, left. The design of the mosque is especially lavish. Exterior and interior are walled with travertine marble quarried in Italy, the exterior marble decorated with carved floral designs. The interior travertine was shipped to England before installation, where passages from the Koran were carved in the Koufic style of calligraphy. The dome and lower roof are covered with buff-colored triangular ceramic tiles. Inside, 1,008 bronze panels are affixed to the dome above a ring of decorated mosaic tiles. Beside the mosque stands a prayer tower, second in height at the airport only to the control tower. The airport job, managed by the Bechtel Company of San Francisco, with HOK designing all the terminal buildings, is within budget and on schedule.

Overleaf, you are looking from the control tower to the mosque, with two of the four public terminals beyond.

216

SOHIO HEADQUARTERS
Cleveland, Ohio

Nearly completed, this will be a big one, 1.5 million square feet of floor space, the largest office building in Ohio. It is under construction on a site bordering Cleveland's old Public Square, across from a tall building that has long characterized the city, Terminal Tower. Terminal Tower has a soaring romantic spire, and the architect declined to usurp its glory by making Sohio taller; he held the height of the new building to 44 floors as against Terminal Tower's 52, and folded his slab of office space into tiers. The bulk of the building was also pulled back to the rear of the site to prevent it from looming over the square. The front is given over to an immense atrium with a skylit garden, shops, and restaurants. Outside is a large plaza, designed at city scale as an entry to the project. In this plaza will stand a tall sculpture by Claes Oldenburg. Further credits, page 230.

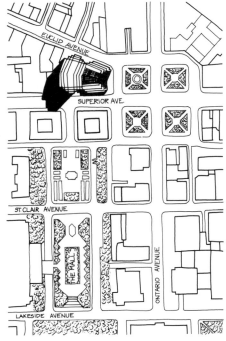

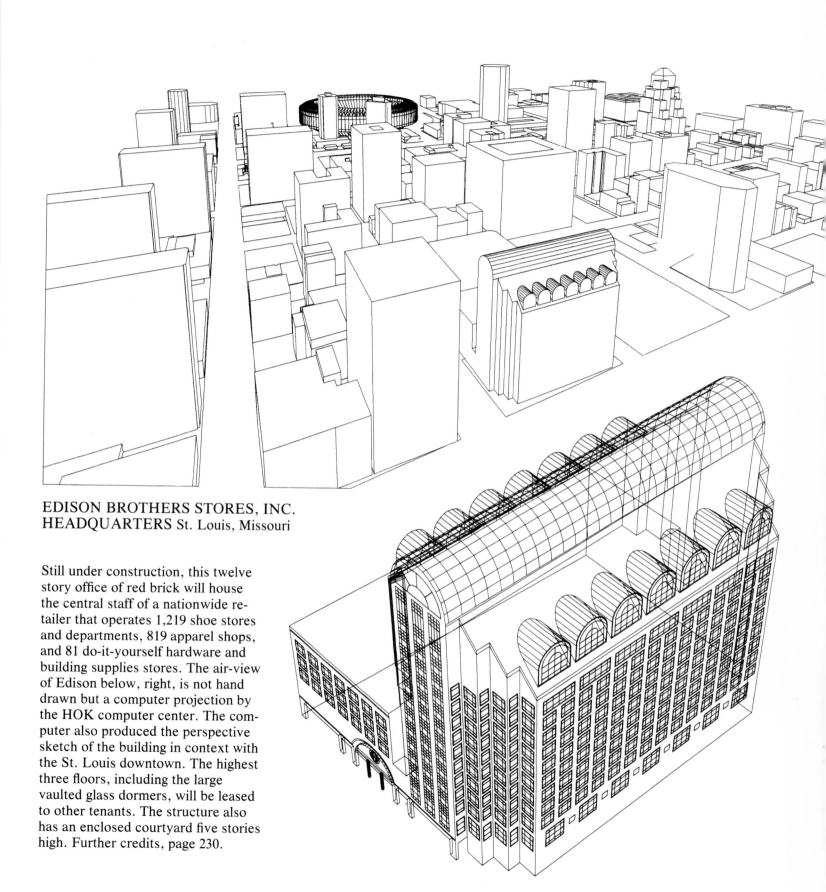

EDISON BROTHERS STORES, INC.
HEADQUARTERS St. Louis, Missouri

Still under construction, this twelve
story office of red brick will house
the central staff of a nationwide re-
tailer that operates 1,219 shoe stores
and departments, 819 apparel shops,
and 81 do-it-yourself hardware and
building supplies stores. The air-view
of Edison below, right, is not hand
drawn but a computer projection by
the HOK computer center. The computer also produced the perspective
sketch of the building in context with
the St. Louis downtown. The highest
three floors, including the large
vaulted glass dormers, will be leased
to other tenants. The structure also
has an enclosed courtyard five stories
high. Further credits, page 230.

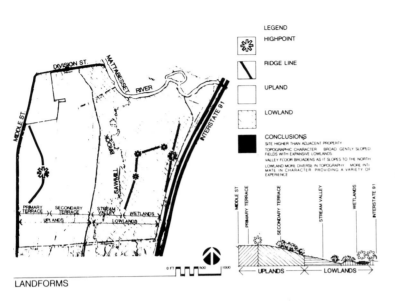

CONCLUSIONS

SITE HIGHER THAN ADJACENT PROPERTY
TOPOGRAPHIC CHARACTER — BROAD GENTLY SLOPED
FIELDS WITH EXPANSIVE LOWLANDS
VALLEY FLOOR BROADENS AS IT SLOPES TO THE NORTH
LOWLAND MORE DIVERSE IN TOPOGRAPHY — MORE INTI-
MATE IN CHARACTER PROVIDING A VARIETY OF
EXPERIENCE

LANDFORMS

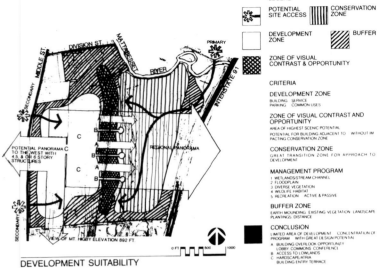

CRITERIA

DEVELOPMENT ZONE
BUILDING   SERVICE
PARKING   COMMON USES

ZONE OF VISUAL CONTRAST AND
OPPORTUNITY
AREA OF HIGHEST SCENIC POTENTIAL
POTENTIAL FOR BUILDING ADJACENT TO   WITHOUT IM
PACTING CONSERVATION ZONE

CONSERVATION ZONE
GREAT TRANSITION ZONE FOR APPROACH TO
DEVELOPMENT

MANAGEMENT PROGRAM
1 WETLANDS/STREAM CHANNEL
2 FLOODPLAIN
3 DIVERSE VEGETATION
4 WILDLIFE HABITAT
5 RECREATION   ACTIVE & PASSIVE

BUFFER ZONE
EARTH MOUNDING EXISTING VEGETATION LANDSCAPE
PLANTINGS DISTANCE

CONCLUSION

LIMITED AREA OF DEVELOPMENT   CONCENTRATION OF
PROGRAM   WITH GREAT DESIGN POTENTIAL
A BUILDING OVERLOOK OPPORTUNITY
   LOBBY COMMONS CONFERENCE
B ACCESS TO LOWLANDS
C HARDSCAPE ATRIA
   BUILDING ENTRY TERRACE

DEVELOPMENT SUITABILITY

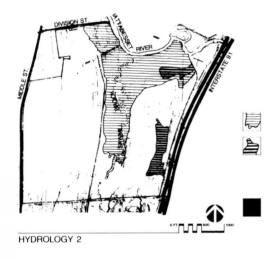

CRITERIA

ANY ALTERATION WITHIN OR USE OF WETLAND OR
STREAMBELT INVOLVING REMOVAL OR DEPOSITION OF
MATERIAL OR ANY OBSTRUCTION CONSTRUCTION
IS CLASSIFIED AS A REGULATED ACTIVITY BY THE AU
THORITY OF MIDDLETOWN

CONCLUSIONS

ALL DESIGN DECISIONS SHOULD PROMOTE THE PRESER
VATION OF SAWMILL BROOK AND ITS IMMEDIATE ENVI
RONS ALONG WITH ASSOCIATED WETLANDS BECAUSE
OF THEIR VISUAL QUALITIES FLOOD CONTROL ABILITIES
AND THE NATURAL WILDLIFE HABITAT PROVIDED IN THEIR
NATURAL STATE

NO STRUCTURE FOR HUMAN USE SHOULD BE BUILT IN
FLOODPLAIN

HYDROLOGY 2

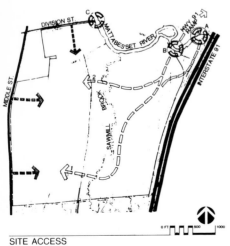

CRITERIA
MIDDLE STREET LIMITED TO SECONDARY ACCESS BY
CITY ORDINANCE

CONCLUSIONS

PRIMARY ACCESS AT N E CORNER OF SITE WITH IMMEDI
ATE PROXIMITY TO HIGHWAY 91 RAMP
BRIDGING OF MATTABESSET RIVER NECESSARY
ROAD THRU LOWLAND HAS GREAT SCENIC POTENTIAL
PASSAGE OVER STREAM CHANNEL AT SOUTH END OF
SITE HAS LEAST POTENTIAL OF FLOODING
DIVISION STREET ACCESS LEAST DESIRABLE BECAUSE
OF LIGHT DUTY CLASSIFICATION AN INDIRECT ROUTE —
AND LOCATION IN FLOODPLAIN

SITE ACCESS

AETNA GROUP DIVISION HEADQUARTERS
Middletown, Connecticut

The client is an insurance company that purchased 287 acres near Hartford and asked the architect to tell them where on the parcel they should be officed, and then to design the building. How HOK's planners go about analyzing a site is shown by the diagrams in the 40-page preliminary report, some of which are reproduced, reduced in size, on the facing page. Landforms, upper left, are important not only for views but for what lies underground, soft soil, for example, or hard rock. Traffic patterns in the public roads of the area count too, as well as possible alternative interior road circulation. Among the total of twelve considerations clearly charted (but not all shown here) are also slopes, micro-climate, vegetation, regional context, soil investigation by borings, visual analysis (views), and utility easements. The overall analysis of all investigations is shown at the bottom of the facing page, with the final design of the building in plan form and, below, under construction. Further credits, page 230.

GALLERIA, DALLAS, TEXAS

On 42 acres of Dallas suburbia, Gerald Hines Properties has opened a different version of its older, enormously successful Houston Galleria. The new Galleria, like the previous one, is an HOK design, and if what happened at Houston is any indication, it should be listed as a project still under way. The Galleria already consists of a three story shopping mall 1,200 feet long, with major multi-story retail stores buttressing the ends: in all, 4 million square feet of space. Also in the first stage HOK designed a 450 room hotel and convention facility, and an office tower. The hotel is the centerpiece of the silhouette, with its vaulted roofs of precast concrete, metal, and glass. Now being completed is a second office building, a twin to the one already built. Further credits, page 230.

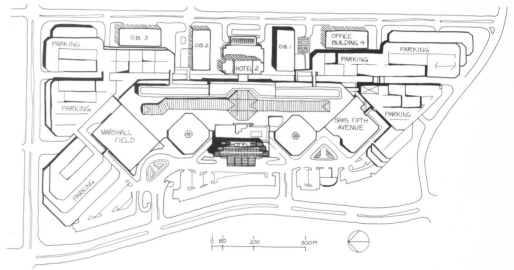

An ice skating rink lies at the heart of Dallas' grand Galleria. Materials of the building group: two different textures of precast concrete with rose colored granite aggregate, gray solar glass, and silver metallic paneling. Accents are of polished granite, mirror-stainless steel, and granite paving.

Above the Dallas Galleria's multi-leveled shopping mall, with its central ice skating rink and its multitude of stores, restaurants, cinemas, and cafes, is a powerfully framed skylight 150 feet in breadth.